EAT PRAY LOVE

Made Me Do It

EAT PRAY LOVE

Made Me Do It

LIFE JOURNEYS

Inspired by the Bestselling Memoir

RIVERHEAD BOOKS

NEW YORK

2016

RIVERHEAD BOOKS
An imprint of Penguin Random House LLC
375 Hudson Street
New York, New York 10014

Introduction copyright © 2016 by Elizabeth Gilbert
Penguin supports copyright. Copyright fuels creativity, encourages diverse voices,
promotes free speech, and creates a vibrant culture. Thank you for buying an
authorized edition of this book and for complying with copyright laws by not
reproducing, scanning, or distributing any part of it in any form without
permission. You are supporting writers and allowing Penguin to continue to
publish books for every reader.

Pages 219–220 constitutes an extension of this copyright page.

ISBN 978-0-399-57677-5

Printed in the United States of America
1   3   5   7   9   10   8   6   4   2

Book design by Amanda Dewey

Penguin is committed to publishing works of quality and integrity. In that spirit,
we are proud to offer this book to our readers; however, the stories, the
experiences, and the words are the respective authors' alone.

CONTENTS

INTRODUCTION

For the past ten years, I've been trying to figure out why *Eat Pray Love* became such a giant phenomenon in the first place. Certainly nothing in my life had prepared me for such monumental success. I'd never been a bestselling author before (I always joke that my first three books had sold "upwards of dozens of copies"), and heaven knows there were already plenty of divorce memoirs, travel memoirs and spiritual memoirs out there on the market before mine hit the bookstores in 2006.

But for some reason, *Eat Pray Love* became a tsunami.

Why?

I've never really known. Whenever interviewers have asked me why I think the book became so popular, my usual answer has been something cheeky and dismissive—something along the lines of, "Your guess is as good as mine, pal!"

But all the while I was shrugging off that question, I was also running into people who kept wanting to tell me stories—stories about how my book had personally inspired or influenced them, stories about how my book had changed their lives—stories, in other words, about what *Eat Pray Love* had made them do. Some of those stories were delightful, some were strange, some were deeply moving. Two of those stories, in particular, have never left me.

Here is the first story I've never forgotten:

One day at a book-signing event in Atlanta, I met an African American woman in her early thirties who seemed positively radiant with happiness. She told me that, a few years earlier, she'd picked up *Eat Pray Love* on the recommendation of a friend. She read it in one sitting. After finishing the last page, she put the book down, stood up from the couch, walked out of her home and never went back there again. It turns out that she had shared that home for ten years with a man who had been physically and emotionally abusing her every single day—but now she was done with it. She left the city, moved back in with her mother, found a new job, saved her money for several years, lost a bunch of weight and (when I met her) had just gotten back from her first trip all alone to Paris. She'd never even gone back to her old home to collect her belongings, and she had never seen her abusive ex-boyfriend again. Her old life was over, never to be revisited. She was an entirely transformed human being.

Here is the second story I've never forgotten:

One day, I received a letter from a woman who wrote, "You'll never believe what just happened because of your book." This woman had read *Eat Pray Love*, and she had enjoyed it, but it hadn't changed her life. Mostly, she'd just liked the travel descriptions and all the details about the food in Italy. But she'd taken the book with her on a family sailing trip that included her older brother. "What you have to understand about my brother," this woman wrote to me, "is that he's a jerk. I love him, because he's my big brother, but he's an arrogant, controlling, entitled jerk." Her brother had been going through a long, drawn-out, expensive and acrimonious divorce. His wife had been trying to leave him for many years, and he'd been punishing her for it— making sure she would suffer dearly for the insult of having walked out on him. He had no intention of ending the battle anytime soon. Then, during this family holiday, he randomly picked up his sister's copy of *Eat Pray Love* and started reading it, mostly as a joke. A few pages in, though, it wasn't a joke for him anymore. He read the whole thing. When he was done with the book, he phoned his lawyer from the sailboat and said, "Call off the dogs." Then he phoned his wife and left her a message saying, "I bless your journey, and I'm sorry." And at last, he let her go.

On the surface, these two people—and these two stories— don't seem to have a single thing in common. Yet I could never forget either, and for years I've been telling them together, in order to demonstrate the impossibly (even bizarrely) wide audience that *Eat Pray Love* has found.

Still, I didn't really know why my book had touched these people specifically, and so many others besides. It was only seeing the incredible range of submissions that came pouring in for this anthology that I finally got it—that I finally saw what those two stories had in common, and why I've been telling them for years. Because at heart they were the same story, the story of a person finally realizing, My life doesn't have to look like this anymore.

The abused woman realized she didn't have to be a victim anymore.

The abusive man realized he didn't have to be a menace anymore.

Both had stepped out of their tired old selves—from one moment to the next—and walked forward into completely new lives. And *Eat Pray Love*, incredibly, had helped them do that. This is what my book is really all about. It was never really about eating pizza in Italy or meditating in India or falling in love in Bali. It wasn't about travel or spirituality or divorce. No, *Eat Pray Love* was about what happens when one human being realizes that her life doesn't have to look like this anymore—that everything (including herself) can be changed. After that realization occurs, nothing will ever be the same again.

That's also the story told by every single person featured in this anthology. Don't get me wrong—these narratives feature an incredible breadth of experience, and they are told in many different voices. But no matter what the background, age or gender of the writer, every single one recalls a moment when he or she realized: "My life doesn't have to look like this anymore." At which point they, too, stepped out of their tired old selves and walked into strange and marvelous new lives.

My friend Pastor Rob Bell has a wonderful definition for the word *despair*. He says that despair is a spiritual condition in which you convince yourself that tomorrow is going to be exactly the same as today. Once you fall into a state of despair, you don't even bother trying to alter anything about your life because what's the point? You become hypnotized by your own stagnation. You resign yourself to sameness because that's what you've tricked yourself into thinking life is: eternal, soul-crushing sameness.

But it's a myth and a lie to believe that tomorrow is going to be exactly the same as today. History and science (and our own lived experience) teach us that we live in a world—indeed, a universe—that is constantly transforming. Not only is tomorrow going to be different from today, the world will be a completely different place an hour from now compared to what it was an hour ago. Look around you: the evidence is everywhere. Everything is shifting. Everything is flowing. Everything and everyone is in a state of becoming. The earth is spinning; the tides are moving; the seasons are unfolding; people are dying and being born (indeed, the cells within your very own body are dying and being born); and God knows that your thoughts never sit still for an instant. The entire story of creation is a story of ongoing change. And the moment you wake up to that story, you realize that you, too, are allowed to change and are allowed to assert agency over the direction you go next. This realization is the beginning of the end of despair. This is what we call resurrection—and it's available at any moment, to anyone.

That's what *Eat Pray Love* was all about, and that's why people responded to it—because it's a resurrection story. And that's what every tale in this anthology is about, too: transformation and resurrection.

It was an incredibly powerful emotional experience for me, reading these essays. I write in *Eat Pray Love* that "one must be prepared for riotous and endless waves of ongoing transformation," but to see those waves rolling in—page after page, wave after wave, change after change—has been pretty amazing.

Search for it, as you read along. You'll see it in every single essay. Search for the moment when each person realizes: "My life doesn't have to look like this anymore." Search for it in yourself, too. That's generally the most interesting moment in anyone's life. Because after that moment? Whatever happens next can quite literally be: ANYTHING.

Onward,

Elizabeth Gilbert

EAT PRAY LOVE

Made Me Do It

Take a Breath

———

Rebecca Asher

The decades of my life can be measured in milestones—the laughter and fearlessness of my twenties, the self-awareness and humility I learned in my thirties and now, the wonder years of my forties.

I can measure those decades because ten years ago, *Eat Pray Love* made me take a breath, and that breath saved my life.

I had been holding my breath for so long. I held my breath waiting for that compliment from boyfriends that never came (gasp). I held my breath hoping to be acknowledged and promoted by a boss who believed I was only so-so (gasp-gasp). I held my breath as I ventured out on my own, determined to be my own boss, only to be met with the second-worst recession our country has ever seen.

I kept gasping for air, and felt like I was drowning.

When I read *Eat Pray Love*, it was a gray Tuesday night. And it happened—that deep inhale, the kind that brings color back to your cheeks and makes your head a little dizzy.

Okay. Okay. Okay.

I took another deep breath and exhaled slowly, grounding myself.

It's time to move, I thought. And I did.

I moved to another state to be near my family. I moved and hustled to find a job, which eventually led to my becoming a freelance writer and author. I put on pretty clothes and remembered how to twirl and dance and caught the eye of a sweet southern boy. I've been breathing and moving ever since. And now, I get to listen to the most amazing breaths of all—those of my two little girls who twirl and giggle, who make me run fast or lie on the floor really still.

At the end of the day, we eat, we pray, we love, and I breathe it all in.

Garden State

Victoria Russell

The first time I opened *Eat Pray Love*, I didn't make it past Italy.

I was fifteen years old and waging war against daily panic attacks. Anxiety had always been with me, but after a year of triggers (bomb threats and lockdowns at school, the death of my grandmother), my usual free-floating, indiscriminate fog of worry crystallized into phobias and then exploded into full-blown panic.

I dreaded trying to fall asleep at night in the dark and quiet; I dreaded waking up and facing the day; I dreaded leaving the house; I dreaded being alone with my racing, reeling mind. The unwelcome thoughts and feelings would come, and I would be off, gasping and crying, fighting for shallow breaths, shaking my leaden hands, pacing on tingling feet.

The only thing worse than the panic was the shame of feeling like I had no right to this suffering. I was not a soldier back from

combat, a refugee in a war-torn country or a terminally ill patient. "You're just weak," a disgusted voice in my head said.

By the start of my sophomore year of high school, I was a
basket case. I barely managed to make it through the first day of
school. That night, I begged my parents not to make me go again.
Months went by before I returned to class. During that time, I
went to therapy twice a week and received home instruction to
complete my schoolwork. I decided not to take medication for
my anxiety, and instead committed myself to learning how to
harness my thoughts. I knew it would be a long, uphill battle,
but the voice in my head that said, "You're weak," began to be
challenged by another voice: "No, I'm not." Slowly but surely, I
was learning how to live with anxiety.

The following spring, I started to read *Eat Pray Love*. Yet as
wise as I was (or thought I was), and as interested in God as I
was, I was also young enough to lose interest when Liz got to
India and the romance of Italy evaporated. The first section of
the book was a crimson sunset; the second section was the cool,
clear night. I was just awakening from my dark night of the
soul—I didn't want to go back yet. I didn't know enough to let
my eyes adjust.

But seven years later, I did.

Now, I was almost twenty-two, freshly graduated from college and feeling like I was about to be swallowed up into a vac-
uum. I had just realized that growing up really does happen to
everyone—and it was happening to me. School, that stable insti-
tution that I had always relied upon, was gone. I didn't know
what I wanted to do next, and I was on the brink of a breakup
with my college boyfriend, who was my first love and best friend.
I heard my old pals, anxiety and panic, knocking quietly but

persistently at the back door of my mind, like they had been patiently waiting there all along.

For the second time, I opened *Eat Pray Love*—and this time, I found a woman who I could relate to. I was finally ready to sit on the bathroom floor with Liz, to join her in the ashram and follow her to the medicine man. When I finished the book, I was giddy with inspiration. I wanted to make decisions. I wanted to kick fear in the face. I wanted to start with the Garden State Parkway.

The Garden State Parkway is New Jersey's yellow brick road (if the yellow brick road were a congested hotbed of aggressive munchkins refusing to use their turn signals). Still, you can get anywhere and everywhere on this multilane, sixty-five-mile-per-hour highway. That summer, I was a license-wielder of five years, and I had still never driven on my home state's biggest road—a source of both shame and inconvenience. I let a phobia of merging at high speed dictate (literally) what paths I could take.

Thanks to *Eat Pray Love*, I decided it was time to put on my ruby slippers and ease on down the Parkway. A dear friend lent me her car and volunteered to sit in the passenger seat (bless her heart). Our destination: Frenchtown, New Jersey, where we would visit Liz Gilbert's store, Two Buttons. With shaking hands, I gripped the wheel, then gritted my teeth, pressed the gas pedal and merged.

When I got into the driver's seat that day, I thought I was at the end of something, that this was a declaration of independence, a breakup with my old toxic flame, anxiety. I returned home smiling and triumphant. I had beaten a full-blown phobia. "Finally," I thought, "I'm over all this fear business."

I was wrong.

I talked a big game to myself and those around me about the importance of being alone and taking risks and following your own path, and even as I did, I was quietly beginning to sink again.

I was determined not to collapse back into paralyzing panic, so instead I became manic. I thought that if I kept moving fast enough, then perhaps I could outrun my fear. If I had passionate affairs, then I wouldn't mourn my lost love. If I took a low-stakes job, I wouldn't have to think about figuring out what I really wanted to do with my life. If I hung out with friends every single night, I wouldn't feel alone. Right?

I jumped from my college boyfriend to a new guy (and then another) faster than I could say "regret." I took a job building longhouses at a local park. *Longhouses.* This stint lasted less than a month, which is longer than the guys hung around. I ran myself ragged with work and play until I was physically ill. I stayed in bed for weeks. I couldn't even look at *Eat Pray Love* sitting on my bookshelf, waiting for me to lovingly thumb through it like I had so many times in previous months.

I felt like I had failed. I had made every mistake in the book—literally. I should have known better. I thought that I could cheat the system, skip the middle, jump straight from the bathroom floor to the beach in Bali. I kept hearing Richard from Texas's voice: "If you want to get to the castle, you've got to swim the moat."

Eventually, I dipped a toe into the goddamn moat.

I ended the relationships that weren't helping my self-esteem. I found a job I loved. I went on a silent retreat at a Benedictine monastery in the Shenandoah Valley. I tried harder, and talked to myself with a softer voice. I made more mistakes. I recognized that, like *japa mala* beads, life is a string of small successes, big failures, love, loss, bravery, fear—all looped together in an infinite circle.

Over time, I learned to listen for what is calling out to me—sometimes in a loud, commanding voice, other times in a whisper. I learned to forgive myself for being scared and imperfect, for making mistakes. I stopped allowing myself to use those mistakes as an excuse to not try new things. Instead, I have to be brave. I have to try.

That's what *Eat Pray Love* makes me do.

The Gift

—

Mallory Kotzman

My mother divorced my father when my brother and I were toddlers, after she had uprooted her life and moved east to accommodate her marriage. She remarried when I was six, to a man eight years her junior, and moved us to a smallish town outside Harrisburg, Pennsylvania, where she set up house with her new husband, a new baby and a slew of in-laws.

Growing up, my mother and I had a tumultuous relationship. She was a bundle of contradictions, soft and pliable one moment, fierce and bold the next. Some days we were best friends, and others, total enemies. Yet the one thing that bonded us for life was reading. Many of my most treasured memories are of being tucked in at night with my mother settled next to me, her smooth butterscotch voice giving life to the characters on the page. The books evolved as I aged; I graduated from the Berenstain Bears to Madeleine L'Engle to S. E. Hinton to Anne Rice, and eventually even Ayn Rand. When I hit adolescence, instead of going shopping, we went to the library. When my mother became the sole breadwinner after my stepfather was injured in a motorcycle accident and I took up the slack by caring for my younger brother, I would retreat to my bedroom every spare moment I had and find solace in the pages of a book.

When I was twenty-three, my mother and I reached a sort of peace. We began to meet for lunch and dig for buried treasure at the local thrift stores—we had the kind of mother/daughter relationship we had always dreamed of. We talked about politics, the latest trends, my itchy feet and always, always books. She mentioned *Eat Pray Love* to me shortly after its release, saying that Elizabeth reminded her of me—no desire to have children, a distaste for marriage but not relationships, and a drive to travel the world. My mother said she couldn't see me living in our town long-term; she told me that she couldn't picture me "settling" anywhere. She just hoped I would find a home base to use as I traveled the world.

I laughed this idea off and tucked it away, along with my dreams of traveling internationally. We lived in a town that people often talked about leaving but rarely did. But I did tell my mother I would buy this book, which had made her think of me. Yet with a hand on my arm, in a serious tone, she told me not to.

"Mallory, don't. I want to buy it for you. It feels like a book I should give to you," she said.

I promised my mother that I wouldn't read it until she gifted it to me.

Not long after, the world caved in. Just when we were beginning to have an honest, adult relationship, my mother was diagnosed with stage IV lung cancer. She was given eight to ten months to live. It was June 2011.

On November 5, 2011, around three a.m., she passed away.

I was devastated. Weeks later, grief-stricken, I found myself in a bookstore. I noticed a copy of *Eat Pray Love*, and I bought it. With a sense of urgency, I went home and read for two straight days. I realized why she had wanted to be the one to give me this book; she was giving me something I had always needed. I read the book a second time, and instead of hearing the author's voice, I heard my mother's. She encouraged me, she believed in me, and, at last, I didn't feel like a black sheep. I wasn't wrong for not wanting children. I wasn't alone in my dreams of traveling. I wasn't the only one who yearned to know God individually. *Eat Pray Love* woke me up. It gave me hope.

This book not only spoke to my soul: it was my mother's last and continual gift to me. Through it, she told me that she knew me, had always known me. That she loved me, and despite what we had been through and what was to come, I was free. The strings were cut. I could finally escape the claustrophobia of small-town life and live the way I wanted to. God had been there waiting, loving and accepting me, and I could choose to love and listen to Him in my own way.

Eat Pray Love showed me that wanderlust is a real and tangible thing. That I don't have to be a mother, despite what society says. It showed me that a relationship could be anything I wanted. Most of all, it showed me that it was a beautiful thing to be myself; to love myself, to define my life any way I chose.

Four years later, that book still means the world to me. I'm married, which surprised everyone—especially me. My husband loves me for all my dramatic eccentricities. His wanderlust matches my own; we get restless if we've been home for more than three months without experiencing something new. He has ambitious personal goals, about which he remains steadfast. He and I currently have no plans for children, but we love our nieces and nephews (honorary and otherwise) with fervor. We define our marriage and our life as we want, encouraging each other to remain individuals, in constant devotion to who we are.

Eat Pray Love brought me through the darkest times of my life. It helped me grow in my relationship with God and taught me to be patient with myself. It made me feel that my mother is supporting me with enthusiasm and pride, enveloping me in her love. She used to say: "At the end of the day, it's just you. So make sure you like the person you're alone with." Her words remind me to not only be honest with myself about where I am, so I can continue evolving as a person I do like to be alone with, but to be honest with my husband as well. I want to create the best marriage I can for us; we both deserve that.

Thank you, Liz. You will never know the courage you gave me simply by giving it to yourself.

Happy Wife, Happy Life

Lisa Becker

E at *Pray Love* made me reinvent my life. I was forty-one, a mother of two, stepmother of two and married to the love of my life when I read Liz Gilbert's memoir. We lived in a beautiful house with an island in the kitchen, a pool in the backyard and roses growing through the white picket fence. After spending more than a decade on the road as a production supervisor in the film industry, and gallivanting around the globe in between projects, I was happy to be a settled-down, stay-at-home mom living my idyllic dream life. Or so I thought.

I'd always felt that I wouldn't be a complete woman if I didn't birth a baby or two. Every palm, tarot and astrological reading I'd ever had showed two kids in my future. They didn't come easy—I had three miscarriages before I had them—but I knew unequivocally that motherhood was my destiny. I just had no idea that it would be the hardest adjustment of my life. I was grateful that my hardworking husband earned a nice wage that allowed me to stay home. Each morning the three of us stood in the doorway for the send-off—my baby boy with his legs wrapped around my waist like a fleshy horseshoe, my four-year-old daughter clinging to my leg like a little chimp, giving one last wave before the bird in the Beamer flew away.

But part of me resented that he was free and I was left to tend to the nest. For more than a decade, I had flown away like that, too, and put in a long day managing a budget and babysitting a crew of a hundred or more. Now my crew was much smaller but, surprisingly, harder to manage. I had been paid well to make important decisions and negotiate deals. Now my only decisions were about where to walk the dog, what to make for dinner and which load to do first, colors or whites. My only negotiations were with little people, small animals and the voices ricocheting in my head. *This is what you wanted*, they chanted, *and you're so lucky to stay home with your babies.* I agreed with the voices and felt the shame rise and the guilt flood over me when I responded, *But it's not enough.* I missed working. I missed being around adults, and I really missed earning a paycheck. I was never ambivalent about wanting a baby; I just hadn't gauged the impact it would have on my life until I was smack-dab in the middle of the motherhood epicenter. How does any woman know how she's going to tackle motherhood until she's put in the game? The thing I'd wanted most in life, what I'd dreamed about for years, had brought me to my knees and made me question my very identity. How could I raise my kids if I was a guilty, spun-out, conflicted mess of a mother?

My husband, who lives by the motto *Happy wife, happy life*, encouraged me to go back to work part-time. But the film industry is an all-or-nothing kind of business. It's not like I could shut my office door and pump. And I was paranoid that my breast milk would end up in the producer's coffee. Still, despite my anxieties, I tried to return to work. But my phone didn't ring and my e-mails weren't returned. I knew what they were thinking; she's a mom now . . . a distracted, hormonal, sleep-deprived shell of her former hardworking, deal-making, whip-cracking self. We like her, but we can get someone who is more focused and won't have to leave early because her kid is sick or her breasts are about to burst.

Like Liz, I had shed many tears in my bathroom in the middle of the night. I was also suffering from postpartum depression. One night, after a three a.m. feeding, I stumbled into the bathroom and began to weep again. I looked in the mirror and saw a depressed, exasperated woman looking back at me. She had oozing watermelon breasts, hair that hadn't been washed in days, teeth that hadn't been brushed and twenty extra pounds clinging to her belly and thighs. Her eyes had big bags and were red and swollen. *"I surrender,"* I sobbed to her. *"I surrender,"* I repeated, this time apologetically. *"I surrender to God. I surrender to motherhood. I surrender the control. I surrender. I surrender. I surrender."* She looked back at me with a steady stare and responded calmly, *"Thank you."*

With my moviemaking career on hold, I started writing again, as a way to unpack the mess in my mind. If chaos is the road to transformation, then I was well on my way. I admitted to myself that I'd been a workaholic and that most of my identity had been wrapped up in my job. If I wasn't working and earning money, then I was pond scum. My career-driven girlfriends confessed to me all the time that they would trade it all for a good man and a baby. In the meantime, they worked nonstop, drove expensive cars, bought designer shoes and slept with their pedigreed dogs. Earning money had made me feel in control of my life, and being financially dependent on my husband had completely spun me out. It had triggered fears and anxieties that dated back to my childhood and were robbing me of my joy of being a mother. It was time to make peace with both my fear over the loss of control and my guilt for not fully embracing my role as a mother. It was time that I reinvented myself.

Eat Pray Love reminded me to love myself first. I must feed myself first before I can give the best of me to those I love. Just as Liz was the administrator of her own rescue, I became the producer of my contentment. Reading Liz's reasons why she didn't want a baby reinforced all the reasons why I did. I decided to surrender to this higher calling and dove into motherhood with a new sense of purpose. I would give motherhood the same balls-out effort I once gave my movie job. I started out as a room mom and became copresident of the PTA. I organized playdates, coordinated school-wide reading events and produced and edited movies for my kids' school and my family.

At the same time, I didn't want to get completely lost in motherhood the way I'd seen some of my girlfriends do—the way Liz had lost herself in men. I adored and respected these women, but their every waking thought, conversation and action was about or for their kids. I promised myself that I would find a new job that was less demanding but still fulfilling and that I would keep writing because it fed my soul. After self-publishing for a couple years, I was officially published in a few literary anthologies. I also started working as an author escort and helped launched a production website for film and television industry professionals.

One day a few years back, we were walking the dog. I was pushing the double stroller, with Jack in front and Scout on the big-sister seat, facing me. Scout always had lots of questions, ranging from Dora to evolution. Today she had a new one.

"Mommy," she asked, "when are you gonna be just a mom?"

"What do mean, just a mom?" I asked.

She elaborated, "You know, like Emma's mom. She's doesn't go to work, and she doesn't go to a writing class like you. She's at school all the time, just being a mom."

I looked at my old soul of a daughter and said, "Never. I'll never be just a mom, because I need more than that to be happy with myself."

She looked perplexed. "You don't like being a mom?"

I cupped her face in my hands, kissed her heart-shaped lips and said, "No, I LOVE being a mom . . . and the fact that I work and I'm a writer makes me a better mother."

She pondered this. "Are you saying you're trying to be a good example for me?"

I laughed. "YES!" I said. "I did not join your life, you joined mine, and it's my responsibility as your mother to show you what's possible . . . to lead by example . . . to support all your passions . . . to teach you how to be creative . . . how to follow your dreams . . . and how to love yourself first."

Intelligence

—

Peter Richmond

For most of my life, I didn't know what to believe in, Big-Meaning-wise, as in: "What're we here for?" Was there an ultimate, original Creator? Or was the explanation for the universe to be found in the realm of physics and particles, with Everything reducible to the Talking Heads lyric, "It's scientific!"?

I wasn't satisfied by either pole. Although baptized and confirmed in an organized religion, from the start I thought the stories in the Bible made for great fiction. Nor was I ever willing to buy entirely into a pure-science paradigm, because, face it: string theory might make scientific sense, and might even be backed by empirical data, but any answer to a question about Being that doesn't address the "Why?" in the equation ain't much of an answer.

To be honest, though, I didn't delve that deeply into trying to find The Truth About Existence. Most of the time, I was too busy trying to make things work out here on earth. By the time I reached the age of fifty, I'd resigned myself to the certainty that we simply weren't equipped with intellects that could even accurately phrase The Question, let alone answer it.

And then, a decade ago, my search for The Answer grew slightly more serious. I'd joined the faculty of a private school, where I taught ninth-graders in an ancient civilization survey class. It was a role that required a diminishment of ego—and a working knowledge of the gods of Egypt, Greece and Rome. In that first year, as the students and I explored the significance of the deities of each civilization, it was hard not to come a little more face-to-face with the eternal conundrum of the meaning of life. And while the thousands of gods who commanded the worship of ancient peoples struck the students and me as engaging cartoon characters (I loved my cat, but, unlike the ancient Egyptians, I didn't worship her), one thing struck me as it never had before: the need for civilizations to invent gods suggested that wanting to find answers was part of our DNA.

The more we studied each civilization's fanciful notions of "the universe," the more I found myself looking, for the first time in a long time, for just a single certainty about existence—a single notion I could wrap my head around.

And then, just before my third year of teaching, during my fifty-fifth year of life, I came across a passage in *Eat Pray Love* and immediately closed the book. Something had finally clicked. Something that made instant, instinctive sense. I was no longer at sea. I was finally, in some measure at least, grounded—well, as much as you can be grounded in the infinite.

Gilbert was describing an experience she'd had in India. She'd been meditating for weeks, waiting for the moment when

that meditation would open the door to some sort of enlightenment, though hardly expecting it to. But it did—whereupon she
was "pulled through the wormhole of the Absolute, and in that
rush I suddenly understood the workings of the universe completely. I left my body, I left the room, I left the planet, I stepped
through time and I entered the void. I was inside the void, but I
also *was* the void and I was looking at the void, all at the same
time. The void was a place of peace and wisdom. The void was
conscious and it was intelligent. . . . It was neither dark nor light,
neither big nor small. Nor was it a place, nor was I technically
standing there, nor was I exactly 'I' anymore."

The void was conscious and it was intelligent.

Instantly, I knew that Gilbert had described the true nature
of being. Maybe it was the "intelligent" part. As the author of
more than a half-dozen nonfiction books, I've experienced some
of my greatest joys in moments—and weeks, months and years—
of learning and discovery.

And so, perhaps it was the notion that after my death I would
not lose my intelligence—rather, it would be amplified beyond
quantification as it melded with the greater Intelligence—that
gave me that moment of surety, clarity and even purpose.

Gilbert gives the void a name: God. I'd prefer, I think, that
this collective consciousness that knows no time or space be
known as We. But godly or not, my belief in its existence carries
some comfort in my remaining days.

The postscript? That third fall semester in ancient civ was a
very different class from the two that had preceded it. As the
study of Egypt began—as Isis, Osiris, Ra, Horus and Bastet introduced themselves in our textbooks—I read that passage of
Eat Pray Love to the class. The notion of an infinite, borderless,

intelligent collective consciousness was, of course, quite new to them. And they dug it.

In the ensuing months, we spent far less time on the stale and boring (to fifteen-year-olds) details of the crop cycles of the Nile or the governance of the Greek city-states, and a whole lot more on how each culture viewed its gods. I'd come to see that teaching students the nature of a culture or civilization through its views of its gods—and, with the appearance of Yahweh in the lores of the kingdom of Israel, its god (singular)—was a far more compelling way of bringing ancient civilizations alive than learning the names of kings, dynasties and battles.

I knew now that the search for a higher meaning in the metaphoric "heavens" is a universal trait. And that taking that path can eventually bring one closer—if one is lucky enough to know of Gilbert's own quest—to, if not enlightenment, a place of comfort.

"Pray" Is the Hard Part

April Schmidt

A few years ago, I was blessed to meet Liz at a book signing in Nashville. I asked her to write the words, "You're welcome," in my worn, tagged, highlighted, cherished copy of *Eat Pray Love*. "You're welcome?" she asked, a bit confused. "Yes," I answered. "Thank you for giving me the courage to change the course of my life."

I always tell people that divorce is really, REALLY hard, but the most difficult part is actually the two years leading up to the divorce, when you go through the gut-wrenching, soul-sucking process of trying to decide whether to hold on or let go. If you have children, as I do, the process becomes more devastating still.

It was during this time that my mother, who is not at all an avid reader, looked at me, full of sadness, and recommended the book. I ignored her—it's what daughters do. A few months later,

I was strolling through Costco of all places, and picked it up on a whim. I devoured "Eat." I clung to every word. I flagged and folded pages; read paragraphs over and over again. Liz got me. Liz *was* me. I wasn't allowed to get a divorce! In fact, I had no right to even be unhappy! This marriage was what I wanted. I had created this life. And to be honest, my husband is a really great guy, so WHAT ON EARTH IS WRONG WITH ME? My own mother even asked me, "Who do you think you are that you deserve more?" I didn't know how to answer that question at the time. But *Eat Pray Love* made me want to find out.

Then I got to "Pray," and decided I was wrong—*Eat Pray Love* was actually the most disappointing book of all time. It started strong, but it lost me. It was difficult to wade through the talk of prayer, chanting, life in an ashram. Devoting days upon days, month after month to meditation, silence, self-discipline, the endless pursuit of God and quest for inner peace—these were concepts I couldn't yet wrap my head around. I put the book on the shelf.

At this point my divorce was well under way, and I had met a man I suspected might be my David (he wasn't my David). I was now fully in the throes of a very deep depression. My mother looked at me once again with even more sadness and suggested I skip to the end, the "Love" part, because I needed to read about something happy. I listened to her, and read "Love" with great fervor. Hope was once again restored. Then, I decided to go back and read "Pray." And again I asked myself, "What is up with this book with the terrible middle?"

Well, of course I didn't like "Pray." "Pray" is the hard part.

I thought getting a divorce was going to cure me of all that made me unhappy. I thought starting over on my own, just my two beautiful boys and me, was the answer. It turns out the joke was on me. It doesn't matter where I live, who I sleep next to, where I work or what I'm doing if I don't feel at peace with myself. *I* was the key to my own happiness.

So I packed my bags, and I went on a journey. In those bags I packed my expectations, my failures, my successes, my losses, my neuroses, my obsessive-compulsive disorder, my anxiety, my anger, my broken heart, my laughter and my love. I marched, bags in hand, right to a therapist's office. On my first visit, the therapist asked if I was truly ready to do this. I told her that I wasn't "ready"—I don't think one is ever truly "ready" to look in the mirror and face the demons staring back at you. But I had no choice. I was going to have to slay those demons and claw my way out of the hole of my depression one grain of sand at a time, or I was going to suffocate and die. It was as simple as that.

I started to read a lot of self-help books. I went back to church after a twenty-year absence. I began to pray. I found God again. In finding God, I learned to let go. In letting go, I learned to breathe. In learning to breathe, I learned to be present. I started to feel lighter. I started a yoga practice. In that practice I found stillness. In that stillness I have grown closer to God, but perhaps more important, I have grown closer to myself.

During this time, I began a relationship with the man I believed to be my Felipe. He turned out to be my David. In many ways, that loss was more painful than my divorce. It seems impossible that a two-year relationship could carry more weight than a fifteen-year marriage, but the truth is, I had attached so much hope and expectation to my David that when it ended, I voluntarily jumped right back into the hole of my depression and had absolutely no intention of ever coming out.

But I reached for my copy of *Eat Pray Love*, complete with its flags and highlights, and I found a friend again. It was as though I could hear Liz's voice calling me from the shelf. Richard from Texas was right! Groceries could love the whole world—or at the very least speak to it. And I was finally ready to listen. I was reminded why I started this journey to begin with. And when I got to "Pray," this time I was ready for it. Not only could I appreciate the work Liz was doing, but I could understand and absorb it, all the blood, sweat and tears. I could do that because I had been through it myself.

My work looked different than Liz's. I wasn't at an ashram in India—I was hiding under my blankets in my bed, refusing to shower and hoping my children were able to get all of their nutritional requirements from ramen noodles. My prayers were different. But I still began to pray, and I never stopped. I learned to meditate. I learned to accept my "monkey mind" because I knew I would never be able to quiet it fully. I found forgiveness and peace.

It's impossible to recount in such a brief space all the things that *Eat Pray Love* "Made Me Do."

But I can say this: it made me take the greatest journey of my life. For many years, my favorite word was *believe*. When I was suffering through that deepest, darkest time of my life, I stopped believing. In love, in hope, in the future, in people and, mostly, in myself. *Eat Pray Love* made me believe again.

Many years ago, I started a blog about life as an autism mom. Thanks to *Eat Pray Love*, I realized I had a lot left to say. I titled my revamped blog, "April's Doorway." *Doorway*, one of my new favorite words. Constantly in movement. Open, shut, swinging, slamming, a window, a peephole, a latch, a lock. A beginning.

Reaching My Boiling Point

Tina Donvito

Why in the world did I think I could do this? I thought to myself as I stared up the steep incline in the middle of the jungle.

Taking an adventure vacation was the latest punishment I'd decided to give my body. I'd read *Eat Pray Love* as I was beginning infertility treatments. Although my goal in life was the complete opposite of Elizabeth Gilbert's (I wanted a baby, she didn't), I found myself dreaming of a life-altering journey like hers that could help me climb out of the black hole of my childlessness. After several years of infertility treatment, shots, surgeries, in vitro fertilization and miscarriages, my husband and I were at a crossroads. There were other things we could try—donor eggs, adoption—but we were never going to have a child that was part me, part him. That possibility was over, and I felt it was my body's fault.

So my husband and I set out for the remote and rugged,

little-touristed Caribbean island of Dominica. This wasn't going to be a lie-on-the-beach-and-drink-all-day kind of getaway. I planned to embark on a physical challenge that would prove my body was capable of accomplishing something. I hoped it was, because this journey wasn't eating or praying or loving (although it involved all three). It was hiking.

Every day, we would be doing challenging treks through the jungle. Although I had enjoyed the occasional jaunt before, I was not a regular-exercise kind of girl. I booked the trip with only a couple of weeks to spare, so I spent what little time I had to train on the stationary bike in our bedroom. But I knew I was woefully unprepared.

I noticed that the local people walked slowly but surely up the steep inclines of the countryside, miles from any town. How could they make hiking look so easy? Still, the first hike I'd planned was a seven-hour round-trip trek to Boiling Lake, the second-largest flooded fumarole in the world and the crown jewel of all of Dominica's hikes. But when I told Nancy, a yoga instructor at our eco-resort, she grew concerned. Visitors to the island shouldn't attempt it on their first day, she said; it was meant to be the hike you worked up to. I started feeling a little scared, but I was determined to stick to my itinerary.

At seven thirty a.m. I was already drenched in sweat. Our local guide, Brother, was missing several teeth and wore thin, worn leather sandals. Our small hiking party of tourists climbed into a pickup truck fitted with eight seats in its bed for the hour-and-a-half drive to Morne Trois Pitons National Park. Mist covered the tops of the craggy peaks, like something out of *King Kong*. The road wound higher and higher into them, until finally we reached the starting point: the pool at the mouth of Titou Gorge.

The first part of the trail was a gentle incline up into the forest. Then the stairs began, a harbinger of the real climbing ahead. But what did I expect of an island with no flat land? I pushed on determinedly, encouraged by my more athletic husband. We descended to Breakfast River, so named because hikers usually stopped here for the first meal of the day. But being already well-fed, we only paused briefly before crossing the stream and beginning a more difficult ascent, all the way to the top of Morne Nicholls.

Short of the peak, a young couple from Guadalupe decided to turn back. If they couldn't make it, how would I? But eventually, huffing and puffing, I reached the summit with the others. Brother presented us with slices of pineapple, which we ate right off the rind. The view across the mountains was lush and green, more like the South Pacific than the Caribbean. I did it! I thought to myself. I climbed a mountain! Except that there was still a long way to go back down.

We made our way down into the Valley of Desolation, where steam rose through vents in the earth, mud bubbled and streams of warm water flowed through a landscape of yellow and orange rocks. We scrambled up over the rocks, staying close to Brother, who knew where it was safe to step, until we emerged above the sunken lake. Sheer cliffs around the rim plunged down to the water, heated to boiling by volcanic cracks in the earth below. Marveling at the sight, I suddenly forgot everything that had happened to me. Although my husband stood next to me, this moment was mine alone. The thought came to me that this lake, like me, was a freak of nature. I had the same bubbling turmoil inside myself, and I was seething with everything that was unfair about my infertility. It was as though I had come face-to-face with my insides.

And then, as if I had drawn strength from this dangerous, beautiful water, I forced my tired legs to work again, with a renewed sense of power. As we made our way back, I remembered what Mount Everest climbers know, that the return journey is the hardest part.

We stopped at a hot spring, where we stripped down to our swimsuits and soaked in a Jacuzzi-like pool. My husband put his arm around me while a gentle waterfall ran over us, as if we were on a romantic vacation instead of in the middle of a grueling physical endeavor. It felt so good, but if we stayed too long our muscles would loosen up too much, so we dried off as best we could with our sweaty clothes and continued on. Now the adrenaline that had propelled me to the lake began to wear off. As we scrambled up and out of the Valley of Desolation, exhaustion began to set in. Brother told me, Every step you take brings you closer. I repeated the phrase like a mantra as I slowly made my way back up the mountain. I had to carry on, I told myself. This was one time when I had control. Finally, I made it to the top.

Now there was just the final descent. I let my walking stick bear my weight with every step down, my legs turning to jelly. When we reached Breakfast River, Brother pulled out a concoction from his pack and rubbed it on my tired muscles. He told me that once, a hiker sprained her ankle and he had to carry her on his back for the whole return trek. Determined not to let that happen to me, I mustered the strength to finish the last part of the hike.

Squeals of delight reached my ears. Local people were swimming in the gorge below. When I reached the pool of Titou Gorge, I tore off my clothes again and plunged into the cool, crystalline water. At the far side of the pool, an opening in the rock led to the gorge. I swam into it alone. Above me, sheer walls of slippery stone wound toward a small, powerful waterfall. The water was clear and deep. I floated on my back and stared up through the trees, the current from the waterfall propelling me back out of the gorge. A sense of calm and peace came over me.

And although the next day I could barely walk, the feeling was still there. I'd done it. I'd made my body accomplish something.

Shift Happens

—

Emily Shaules

Have you ever picked up a book and felt like it was written just for you? How about one that literally saved your life?

My health problems began during my senior year in college. What started as terrible stomach pain led to surgery to remove my gallbladder. When that didn't alleviate my symptoms, I was sent for test after test. Finally, I was diagnosed with ulcerative colitis and irritable bowel disease. I went back for my last semester armed with a bunch of drugs, pleased that I'd lost those last fifteen pounds, thanks to not being able to eat solid foods over the break. Law school flew by, and the meds kept my problems in check. I met a wonderful man and fell in love. We were seemingly perfect together—same upper-middle-class background, same interests, same sense of humor. There was this pesky detail of him wanting to be a father more than anything in the world, and me really not wanting kids, but I was sure that would work itself out.

A week after graduating from law school, I felt a snap in my neck like whiplash while my boyfriend and I were making love. I was told in the emergency room that I had pulled a muscle and would be better in a few days. Only I wasn't. The pain increased and gradually spread throughout my entire body. Within months, I was diagnosed with fibromyalgia and told I would be in pain for the rest of my life. I was twenty-five.

I refused to let my illnesses slow me down. I took the bar exam in a neck brace, with a bottle of Vicodin by my side. I passed on my first try, and started practicing. My boyfriend and I got married and adopted the cutest dog alive. We were well on our way to the 2.2-kid, white-picket-fence lifestyle we'd been raised in. But my body just wouldn't keep up. I was fired from my job because I couldn't handle the firm's "reduced" schedule of forty hours a week, let alone the normal eighty-hour one. Then came another job and another termination. These apparent failures were almost too much to bear for a lifelong straight-A student and perfectionist.

When my husband was offered a sixteen-month stint in London, we thought our prayers had been answered. I could rest and heal while he worked. But I felt useless in London. I sat around all day, watching TV and smoking pot to manage the pain, and he worked long days. Soon our relationship started to crack under the strain.

Back home, all our friends were on their first or second child. We no longer had the excuse of living abroad—we had to catch up. I couldn't admit to my husband—or maybe even to myself—

that I was looking for a way out. Briefly I thought I'd found the answer in a chick-lit book titled *Baby Proof*, which told the story of a couple who had decided not to have kids—until the husband changed his mind. But when it ended with the wife discovering that a child was indeed what she wanted, I literally threw the book across the room. Wasn't there anyone out there who was happily child-free?

Enter Liz Gilbert. I bought *Eat Pray Love* in the airport when we were on our way to visit my husband's family and hid it in my suitcase, paranoid that my motives for reading it would be transparent if it were discovered. Within ten pages, I knew this was *my* book. When I read the passage where Liz prays in the bathroom, I felt as if someone had been spying on me.

Reading the book gave me hope that I, too, could create a life I truly wanted to live, instead of settling for the one that had been predetermined for me.

On a Monday night, I told my husband that there was no way I could have kids. On Tuesday, he asked for a divorce. It was the scariest thing I'd ever done. Too sick to work more than ten hours a week at a legal aid nonprofit, I knew I wouldn't be able to support myself. But more than that, I was losing my best friend, the man I thought I would grow old with.

One week later, at a routine checkup, I discovered I was pregnant. At first it seemed like a sick joke, but then I suspected it was God's way of seeing if this was really the choice I wanted to make. I had an abortion. Recovering in our bedroom at home, without my soon-to-be-ex-husband knowing, was the lowest point of my life. I moved out and within a few months started a support group for fibromyalgia sufferers, where I learned about healing with raw foods. Within a week of going raw vegan, I felt better for the first time in years, and within four months I was off all of my meds. I haven't been back on them since. I retired from the practice of law and moved to Asheville, where I became an actor and started my own company, Shift Bars. We sell the world's first zero-glycemic raw organic vegan energy bar made with zero-glycemic sweeteners. I discovered the Law of Attraction and Abraham-Hicks, and learned that I do, indeed, create my own reality. Today, I am surrounded by people who love me for exactly who I am. I'm so grateful for the second chance I created for myself by listening to that small, still voice inside. *Eat Pray Love* gave me the courage to act on what it said.

I look back upon those years spent suffering and realize my body was doing its best to protect me from taking a path that I didn't want to be on. Each milestone in my younger years was accompanied by pain, as if my body were trying to ask me, "Are you sure you want to do this?" but I was always too stubborn to hear. Now, I listen closely. My ex-husband is remarried and has the children he longed for; I remain grateful to him for the part he played in my life. My experience with him allowed me to recognize the power I have within: the power to create the life I want.

Thank you, Liz, for unabashedly sharing your story. It inspired me in ways I will never be able to express with words alone.

Making Peace with Myself

Eduardo Martinez

I n September 2000, at the age of twenty-eight, I made what I thought would be the most important commitment of my life. After years of courtship (I needed to be sure it was true love), I decided I was finally ready to take the leap. I was entering Roman Catholic seminary. I was going to be a priest.

I met a man at the start of my second year. He was handsome, and we had many things in common, including love and devotion for our overbearing Hispanic mothers who dreamed of being able to say they had priests for sons. Soon, we discovered something else we shared, and that we were both trying to escape: homosexuality.

Shortly after, I began having doubts about my vocation. A life of chastity and poverty suddenly seemed far less appealing. It didn't help that all the seminarians I lived with first appeared to be saintly men and then quickly morphed into a bunch of normal guys who'd flood the toilet on a regular basis by using too much toilet paper. I thought these men would mirror those I had read about in *Lives of the Saints*. Instead, it turned out that the image I had created of them—and of myself—was just that, an image.

When the sex-abuse scandal within the Catholic Church became global news, I knew it was finally time for me to leave. Holy Mother Church and I both had issues of our own to sort out. I'd put so much of my identity into the idea of being a priest that I hadn't stopped to think: what does it mean to be in hiding as a gay man? How would I ever feel fulfilled, religiously or personally, if I was unable to be myself?

So I left seminary to pursue my education and live as an out-and-proud gay man. And I did just that, spending the early part of my thirties catching up on lost time by hitting the nightclub scene and dating as many men as possible, all while working on my undergrad degree in literature. By October 2007, I had finished my first teaching credential and started working on a graduate degree in education. I was well on my way to creating an intellectual and stimulating career, but something was missing.

I spent so many years searching for my identity, first at seminary, and then in school and at clubs, but in my thirties I finally realized: it didn't matter how many versions of myself I tried on if I never devoted any time to cultivating who I really was and what I really wanted—not just what I thought I should want. What's more, by the time I felt ready to really love someone—and demonstrate that love in a healthy way—I had no understanding of how to do it. I had hidden it for too long, and now it was raw and unmanageable and manifested itself as obsessive compulsion. It was too much for any romantic prospect to handle.

Come year's end, I was on a career high but my heart was completely shattered. I was such a mess that I soon became a frequent visitor of the self-help section of local bookstores. I read plenty of books in the ensuing months, but it wasn't until I read *Eat Pray Love* that I decided to take action. I needed to make a change, and it needed to be about me, about discovering my true self.

My parents had recently retired to Arizona and were renting out their house in California, the house I was born in. It was between tenants at the moment, which was perfect. I realized I could turn the house into my own private sanctuary and use it as a way to make sense of all the past decisions I had made—good and bad. Instead of Italy, Bali and India, I would visit my past, my heart and God.

There were several rules I had for myself during the year I ended up renting the house: no TV, no bringing work home and no wild parties. Instead, I'd come home, light candles, burn incense, journal and pray. I practiced this ritual for an entire year. In that time, I learned the art of meditation and reestablished my relationship with God based on the experiences I'd had since leaving seminary. In my journal entries, I allowed myself to express my romantic longing and made peace with my homosexuality.

Ever since reading *Eat Pray Love*, I've been on my own spiritual journey, determined to figure out who I really am and what I really want out of life. The one thing I've learned for sure is this: the more I search, the more I evolve. I intend to keep exploring.

Imperfectly Enlightened

Shannon Sykes Westgate

I purchased *Eat Pray Love* in 2007, and for several months it sat patiently by my bedside, waiting to be read. Then, late one Thursday night at the end of October, I received a phone call that my husband had been arrested for driving under the influence. He was pulled over for a headlight issue and found to have been drinking. Unfortunately, unbeknownst to me, this was not his first offense; he had similar trouble much earlier in his life. I was floored. We had been married for two years. This threw me into a "what have I done" moment.

While my two little boys slept peacefully in their beds across the hall, I sat, tears streaming down my face, feeling more alone than I ever had in my life. Then I reached for *Eat Pray Love*. I stayed up all night reading and finished just before the sun rose. Over the next few days it became clear to me that, like Liz, I had lost myself and needed to refocus on what would bring me back.

The next year was spent dealing with the fallout of my husband's mistake. He ended up serving time over the summer. He had work release and would come home just after I left for work and return before I could get home. We wrote to each other every day, sharing our thoughts and feelings about what we were experiencing. It ended up being a transformative time in our relationship and helped us to grow stronger. He gave up drinking and hasn't touched a drop in eight years.

In 2009, I decided to commit the entire year to doing things that challenged and scared the hell out of me. I needed to get out of my comfort zone and learn what I was truly capable of.

First, I registered to walk in the Susan G. Komen 3-Day, a sixty-mile walk for breast cancer. I registered solo and trained tirelessly. Completing the walk was a tremendous victory for me as I had fought weight issues for years. The entire event was inspiring, only made more so because I was now in the best shape of my life. For the first time, I felt like a powerful woman surrounded by other powerful women.

Next, I registered to spend a week in meditation practice with Jack Kornfield at the Omega Institute for Holistic Studies in Rhinebeck, New York. As I trained for the walk, I would listen to Jack for hours. His way of explaining the tenets of Buddhism made them feel accessible and easily applicable to my life. I was finally about to meet my guru.

There was a problem, though. As a lifelong introvert and victim of severe self-judgment, preparing for the Omega retreat brought up all sorts of insecurities for me. I didn't know what to pack. I didn't want to look like I was trying too hard. I didn't want people to know I was a fraud. I was certain all the other attendees would be seasoned meditators and, thanks to my non-yogi-like attire, I would immediately be identified as an amateur.

When I arrived, though, I found that most of my anxieties were completely off base. The positive energy immediately put me at ease. The people surrounding me were welcoming, warm and open, not at all the judgmental barbarians my mind had conjured. Upon arrival, I met a fellow retreat goer and found common ground even before the retreat began. I was going to survive this adventure. I settled in to the first guided meditation and was ready see where this could take me. Jack was everything that I had hoped, and I had an opportunity to share with him my gratitude for his teachings.

There *was* one aspect of the retreat that proved to be cause for anxiety—and that I hadn't even known to be anxious about. This is why you always need to read the brochure for these things! The retreat was silent. Somehow, I had completely missed this when registering. By the time I reached the third day, I felt like I was losing my mind. I would go back to my cabin and cry. I wanted to go home, away from the isolation and all the demons it raised for me. It was as if a highlight reel of all the mistakes and misconceptions I had ever made was on constant loop in my mind. But I was stuck on this campus, there was no Internet connectivity or cell phone service to be had and my fears had me cornered. I had no choice but to face them head-on.

My ability to persevere despite these fears became transformative. I remember leaving the retreat feeling gratitude and love for everything and everyone around me, and for the first time I was able to expand that circle to include myself as well.

Eat Pray Love gave me the courage to embark. Without Liz's account of her own flawed journey, I never would have thought I could attend a meditation retreat, something that seemed reserved for only perfectly enlightened beings, one of which I was certainly not. From Liz, I learned that it was never too late to start again. I forgave my indiscretions and granted myself the permission to create the life I now understood I deserved. With my newfound clarity, serenity, gratitude and joy, I was able to find my way back to my heart. My relationship with my husband flourished, and I had a terrific appreciation for every moment I spent with my children and family. I felt renewed and ready for big changes.

One day, after coming home from a particularly tumultuous day at work, I knew it was time. I could not wait another moment. I had no idea what it was, but the pull had become too strong to ignore. I began searching the Internet for potential business acquisition opportunities in Michigan. I was looking for a business I could call my own. Almost immediately I saw a family-owned resort in northern Michigan for sale. Now mind you, my profession was in integrative medicine practice management and my education was in interior design. Running a resort was not something I had ever considered, but I knew I had to see the property.

My husband and I arrived in the charming coastal town of Arcadia and met the couple who owned the resort. They were hospitable and very down-to-earth. As I walked the grounds, I felt a peace come over me. I felt as though I was home. Later, when I shared the experience with a friend of mine, she said, "It is as though your soul was already there and your body just had to catch up with it." The next morning, walking on the beach with my husband, I said, "If this could work, I cannot imagine how I could say no to it."

Today I turn forty-five. I am sitting at the kitchen table, which is mission control for my beloved resort. My life has morphed into the life I know I was meant to lead. It is not idyllic, but it is perfectly imperfect every day. I once saw a quote: "Your job is the excuse through which you get to love people." This completely encapsulates how I feel about what I do. I am thrilled to be able to serve my guests and share my little corner of paradise, all the little things about Arcadia that bring me joy. I live from my heart and have gratitude for all that life brings. To Liz, my guide in creating a life of authenticity, I am forever grateful.

There You Are

—

Jan Haag

"Remember what our Guru says—be a scientist
of your own spiritual experience. You're not
here as a tourist or a journalist;
you're here as a seeker. So explore it."

—RICHARD FROM TEXAS, *Eat Pray Love*

My husband, a newspaper photographer, died sitting in a
massive Arts and Crafts–style oak chair he'd made in
our garage. His sister, a costumer for a major film-
maker, helped him sew the leather cushions on her industrial
machine. A community college journalism instructor and newspaper adviser, I was in my office at school when I got the call
from the coroner's office. That day I learned that coroners don't
call you to wish you a good day and, long before the tears came,
that my universe had toppled in on itself.

It was a complicated marriage; aren't they all? By the time he died, seventeen years into it, we were living in different towns, though we saw each other on weekends. Most of his coworkers thought he was divorced. We weren't. We still owned a house together, shared a dog. We loved each other; we were family and stayed that way. He was forty-eight years old; I was forty-two.

I spent the next few years taking bits of his ashes in plastic film containers to places he'd loved, to places he'd wanted to go, to places I wanted to go. I deposited them quietly, illegally, in water, in earth, in the mulchy detritus of fall leaves, in snow and once, as close as I could get to slowly creeping lava on a big island in the middle of the sea. I stood and watched as Madame Pele gently surrounded him with thick, steaming fingers, then oozed over him, making him part of her.

I came to think of him as my companion spirit, always with me. Sometimes I'd walk in the house and smell him, and I'd say what he used to say when he heard my voice on the phone: *There you are.*

I took a trip with some of his ashes up the coast of British Columbia, on a small paddle wheeler that looked as if it had just starred in a production of *Showboat*; the captain announced that we were going to see a ghost town. I'm a Californian; I immediately thought of crumbling cabins tilting into deserts, the lone tumbleweed bouncing through the parched scene. But this was land black with old trees, flowing ribbons of dark sea and, over it all, sky so blue it looked like crayons right out of a fresh box. And even from the water, I could see that the tiny town of Ocean Falls was no ghost town. There were people on land, and cars, and on a hill a rose-colored house beaconed its way into my brain. Out of nowhere, a voice in my head began to relay a story: *My mother painted our house bright pink the summer I turned ten, in a fit of creativity.*

I've been writing since I could hold a pencil; I know a fictional character when I hear one. I went to my cabin on the boat and got pen and paper, began scribbling what I heard and saw. In that moment a novel was born.

The next summer I went back with my new partner and his camera. We flew in on a float plane, landed on the saltchuck (a mixture of fresh and salt water) and explored the town, which smelled like pines and the sea. We learned about its history as a once-thriving mill town that housed five thousand people at its peak, now mostly empty, the old paper and pulp mill a hull of its former self. It rained for all five days we were there; Ocean Falls turned out to be the wettest spot in western Canada.

I came home with lots of notes and interviews, with characters and the story of a town the government attempted to bulldoze and burn down before its remaining residents got the destruction stopped. Then I stopped, too. Intimidated, terrified of what lay before me. The responsibility I had taken on to tell this story—which no one had asked me to tell, no one had offered to publish—overwhelmed me.

I put all my Ocean Falls material away and went back to my job, resigned to being "just a teacher."

Until *Eat Pray Love* showed up. I, like millions of others, fell in love from the first pages, with Liz Gilbert's voice and her story. It wasn't my story exactly, but it was a good one, the very best kind. Immediately I grabbed a pencil and started underlining, because she was talking to me. Richard from Texas was talking to me, too, when he said: "Someday you're gonna look

back on this moment of your life as such a sweet time of griev-
ing. You'll see that you were in mourning and your heart was
broken, but your life was changing."

I realized then that my heart was still broken from the loss of
my husband; that all our hearts get broken in the process of
these messy, imperfectly perfect lives. But I also knew how grateful I was for the circumstances that led to that heartbreak—for
the huge, love-filled, life-changing events that made me, well,
me. As Felipe tells Liz in the book: "This is a good sign, having
a broken heart. It means we have tried for something."

And I knew that was true, too. That I had walked imperfectly through a marriage, that I was, as Liz learned from the
Bhagavad Gita, living this life in my own awkward, stumbling
way. I had tried. I was still trying.

So I opened my heart to the voices inside, went back to
Ocean Falls two more times, did more research, more interviews. I found myself ready to put on the page stories of trees
and a town surrounded by mountains and water, inaccessible by
road, a small place with people who lived and loved and died. I
was helped in this by a writer who didn't know me, but whom I
felt somehow I knew, who chronicled her journey to reclaim her
heart by traveling to Italy, India and Indonesia. Her book had
helped me to reclaim my heart, too. She'd helped me to find the
confidence to write three drafts of a historical novel, though I
didn't have a publisher waiting for it. Because it was a story I
wanted to tell. It showed up on the page, under my typing fingers: *There you are.*

It took me years to write. It found an agent who loved it. It's
had more than two dozen rejections, but we keep trying. I've
revised it more than once, each time grateful for the chance to

create another version of it. Which, as *Eat Pray Love* reminded me, we do every day, creating anew with, if we are lucky, big love and thankfulness and surprises—lots and lots of surprises.

I look upon this process as a great adventure. I have tried for something. The writing, the research, the travel to this out-of-the-way place has changed me. My broken heart has healed, even though you can still see the cracks if you look closely. My companion spirit has been joined by others, some of them fictional, all of them alive within me. I am ready to be delighted by what comes next.

Adventurous Woman

Laurna Strikwerda

When I first read *Eat Pray Love*, it completely freaked me out. As a twenty-seven-year-old woman, I didn't just read it as Liz's story—I read it as a story about what I was supposed to want. I was supposed to want to be adventurous.

I'm sure that scaring impressionable twenty-seven-year-olds was the last thing that Elizabeth Gilbert ever wanted to do when she set out to write a memoir about finding her own fine self. I imagine she wanted to tell her story, and if it resonated, great. But her story became bigger than her—it became a story about what it means to be a young woman with infinite choices and possibilities. Why would you keep doing what women have done for centuries if you could chart your own course? Why would you do what your mother or your grandmother had done, and be tied down to one place, if you could be on a plane to the next bit of unknown territory?

I remember my mother talking about being one of the first women in her small Christian college to go on to graduate school, let alone travel to France to do her research. At the time, such a decision was considered a huge step into the unknown. But I'm a member of the *Eat Pray Love* generation of women, and I felt I was expected to do more than that.

I did travel. I visited several countries in college, making my way slowly around the globe with twenty-five other classmates and a professor. I spent a summer in Yemen learning the back alleys of old Sanaa and later made a handful of work trips overseas.

But no matter how many places I went, it never felt like I was being truly adventurous—not *Eat Pray Love* adventurous, at least. Granted, I lived in Washington, DC, which is the one-upping, adventuring capital of the young and professional world. I knew that in reality, only a tiny percentage of America's population and an even tinier percentage of the world's population—especially its women—have the opportunity to get on a plane and travel for work or leisure; that the vast majority of the other humans on this planet are more focused on getting food on the table and keeping a roof over their heads than acquiring air miles. But I often forgot this reality when I was surrounded by my own little sliver of the universe, filled with other women-who-were-more-adventurous-than-me. Other women who knew where to get manicures in Benghazi and what to do when your satellite phone stopped working in the Sahara and how to find an authentic Mexican restaurant in Hong Kong. Women who weren't tied down; who had more than one passport, spoke more than one language, had more than one home.

They were the exciting ones, I thought.

Maybe if I traveled once a year. Maybe if I lived abroad for a whole year. Maybe if I lived abroad for two years. Maybe if I traveled and then wrote a book. Maybe then I would be exciting enough to merit the title "adventurous woman." But until that point, I knew it—I was boring.

And for five long years, I beat myself up for this.

Until one day, when I made my peace with adventure. It happened accidentally, when I was traveling—yet of course still feeling unadventurous.

In the spring of 2015, I went to Spain to walk for a week on the Camino de Santiago, the medieval route that has been used for centuries by pilgrims demonstrating their devotion, and now by spiritual seekers looking for renewal.

Ever since I studied medieval art in college, walking the Camino had been a dream of mine. I loved the idea of a moderately sized adventure, one that was about walking, not running, and still had the safety of towns and sleeping on mats on the floor instead of inside tents. I set off with underprepared feet, too much in my backpack, thirteen words of Spanish and my copy of *Eat Pray Love*. I hadn't picked the book up in years and wanted to come back to it and see if it was still the same story I remembered.

I was going to be walking the Camino with a friend. Not just any old friend, but a Washington, DC, friend who had moved to Europe to become an entrepreneur and then proceeded to climb Mount Kilimanjaro, sail the Mediterranean and take up rock climbing. In short, an adventurous person.

After the first day, my friend and I decided to walk separately at our different paces. She would bound off each day, blister free, minimalist backpack bouncing, and meet a stranger, who would become an instant best friend.

I, meanwhile, was forcing my swelling feet to take just one more step while walking alone, usually too nervous to strike up a conversation with a stranger.

At the end of the third day of this, after trying to bandage blisters in a field, getting lost (despite the enormous yellow arrows that populate the entire Camino) and then succumbing to a taxi instead of staying on my feet, I crumbled.

"I feel so small," I said that evening at our hostel, curled up on a mat. "I'm a slow walker, I overpacked, I can't connect with anyone. I have to face it . . . I'm just not adventurous."

My friend sat down next to me. "Hey," she said. "I'm just walking—I'm not having an adventure. You're hauling your ass all over this Camino. You're not giving up. *You're* having a freaking adventure."

I didn't fully process this concept until I was on my way back to the States. A few thousand feet over the Atlantic, I began to unpack this idea I had held, unquestioned, for so long. Was having an adventure really about doing the most daring, bold, energetic thing? Was it about having stories to tell at cocktail parties? Was it about freedom and travel and not being tied down? Or did it have something to do with your own heart and your own courage, in whatever form that came?

On that plane ride home, I read *Eat Pray Love* through a different lens. I read it as one woman's story about listening to her own voice, and where that decision led her.

This time, the passage that most spoke to me was the one about Liz's stay in Italy. "*I have put on weight*," she wrote. "I exist

more now than I did four months ago. I will leave Italy notice-
ably bigger than when I arrived here. And I will leave with the
hope that the expansion of one person—the magnification of
one life—is indeed an act of worth in this world. Even if that life,
just this one time, happens to be nobody's but my own."

I realized there was one adventure I had never tried: self-
acceptance. I had spent so much time thinking about what I was
supposed to be doing, going to, or experiencing, that I had
hardly ever managed to hear my own voice. I had hardly managed to see that even if I was walking more slowly, I was still
covering ground.

When I returned from the Camino, I joined a neighborhood
association and my church council. I knew that I wanted to
travel again, but I also wanted to feel rooted in the place that I
live; I wanted to hear the voices and stories of my neighbors. I
craved what many other women before me had resisted—a sense
of being connected to a particular place, to family and community. That was where the weight of my life was pulling me.

Thinking of *Eat Pray Love* now, perhaps Liz didn't necessarily set out to be adventurous or to be free. I wonder if she simply
tried to find her own voice, and that search happened to take her
around the world. Listening to my own voice led me deeper into
my own neighborhood instead. And that's fine. What matters
most is paying attention to that inner voice and trusting that it
has something to say. That's what *Eat Pray Love* made me do—it
made me trust mine.

Tell the Truth, Tell the Truth, Tell the Truth

Eran Sudds

I remember this moment vividly. It was, after all, my *Eat Pray Love* moment. I was twenty-seven years old and curled up on the kitchen floor, uncontrollably bawling my eyes out because I couldn't face the fact that my dishwasher needed to be unloaded again.

Yes, you read that right. I was sobbing my heart out on the floor all because this miraculous modern-day machine had produced yet another batch of perfectly clean dishes and I was going to have to unload them and put them away. Again.

I know—complete First World problems.

Yet my dishwasher seemed to perfectly personify the meaninglessness, repetitiveness and utter emptiness that was my life at the time.

Sure, I looked good on paper. I had a decent job doing something I was really good at. I had a cute little house, an ambitious, handsome and supportive husband, two cats and the aforementioned dishwasher. But I was empty.

Shortly after my dishwasher-induced meltdown, I picked up my dog-eared, well-loved copy of my own personal bible, *Eat Pray Love*, and started reading it again. Except this time, it was different. This time, I tingled in anticipation. You see, I knew a change was brewing and that it was all going to start when I stopped living my life for other people and started living for me.

Within a matter of days, I had given two weeks' notice at my job, even though I had absolutely no other plans besides hopping on a plane to Australia with my husband to visit friends. My co-workers were shocked. Why was I quitting? Didn't we need the income? Had I found another job?

I had no answers for them. All I knew was that I wasn't happy, I had a billion things I wanted to try and time was ticking.

But after five years of intense soul-searching, self-discovery and career exploration, I still felt lost. My husband and I were starting to feel the pressure to start a family (neither of us was getting any younger), but I just didn't feel comfortable taking that leap yet. I had one last, BIG dream I wanted to fulfill.

A few years prior, my husband and I had taken a three-week road trip through France. I had always felt like a piece of me belonged to this country, and this road trip in our peppy little Fiat only solidified the feeling. When we stopped in Bordeaux for a night, I knew immediately that one day I would return. And ever since, my heart longed to go back. I wanted to be enveloped in the language and the culture, and I wanted to feel like

I knew that city the way it seemed to know me. I knew that if I could go back there, by myself, I would be able to figure everything out.

I also knew that once I had a baby, the likelihood of me going back, especially by myself, was incredibly slim. So I booked a flight to Bordeaux and planned a four-week-long hiatus from my life and everyone in it.

I rented a quaint French apartment with perfect French windows. I systematically devoured all the self-help books and became one with my copy of *Eat Pray Love*. I drank copious amounts of cheap French wine and ate an embarrassing amount of chocolate croissants. And when I left that gorgeous city, I was completely certain of Who I Was. I totally had my shit together, and I was cocky as all get-out about that fact.

Soon after returning from that trip, I launched a new photography business. I had very little photographic experience and was practically clueless as to how to work a camera, but I knew in my heart that I could take a great photo. I also knew that taking a photograph of someone and making that person feel beautiful was something I wanted to experience as much as I possibly could.

So at thirty-two years old, I was set. I knew myself inside and out. I had figured out my career path (finally!). It was time to start Phase 2: Making Babies.

Everyone always says, you're never really 100 percent ready to be a mother. But, like I said, I was feeling pretty cocky. After all, I had just spent the last five years in deep self-exploration. I had had my *Eat Pray Love* moment on the kitchen tiles. I had taken my *Eat Pray Love* trip to Bordeaux. I was pretty confident that nothing could shake this rock-solid identity of mine.

And then motherhood, hand-in-hand with postpartum depression, hit me like a truck. A giant, red, 18-wheeler truck. Head-on. With thunder and lightning bolts. And a sound track of depressing, angry, heavy metal music, screaming, YOU'RE NOT GOOD ENOUGH TO BE A MOTHER!

I was completely unrecognizable to myself. Gone was the girl from Bordeaux with the big plans and even bigger dreams. Gone was the cockiness and self-awareness.

In its place was a giant, gaping hole. With a cute, frustrated baby in the middle who just wanted to be loved by his mama.

In the months that followed my son's birth, I would think back to my *Eat Pray Love* days in Bordeaux, and it felt like a dream. I didn't know what to do to get back to the way I was or how to possibly reconcile this new life of motherhood with that past life of self-awareness and joy.

To be honest, I was mad at *Eat Pray Love*. I was mad that Elizabeth Gilbert had tricked me into creating a life I loved. I was mad that I had had a taste of perfection and then it was all shattered by the arrival of this tiny human being. I was mad that I hadn't chosen Liz's life of no children. But I was also mad that I loved my son so hard and that there was no way I was giving him up.

I was MAD at *Eat Pray Love*.

But I picked it up again anyway. I picked it up because I felt like I had nowhere else to turn. I flipped to all those dog-eared pages I had loved so deeply and I found that the words no longer spoke to me. The passages I had underlined no longer gave me those old feelings of hope and anticipation. They felt dead.

So, I started at the beginning. I read that first page, "Tell the truth, tell the truth, tell the truth," and suddenly I knew what I needed to do. I needed help. I needed to be honest with myself and all the people who loved me. I needed to start living my life for myself again. *Eat Pray Love* had shown me the way once before, when I needed it most. There was no reason it couldn't now.

What I did next wasn't a huge, life-altering act. I didn't run away. I didn't leave my husband or my baby. I picked up the phone and called a postpartum depression help line. And I told the truth.

Two years later, on this past Mother's Day, I held a photography-based fund-raiser for the Pacific Post Partum Support Society, the organization that helped me get back on my feet. I offered photo sessions to moms and their kids, with all proceeds going back to the organization. A total of 108 mothers participated, and all of the moms were given the opportunity to pose with their beautiful children and hold a sign with a message like, "You are a good mother," or "You deserve to be celebrated." I called it the Good Mother Project.

The mothers who participated started talking to me. Some told me stories of how they had struggled with postpartum depression; others told me about their isolating experiences with a colicky baby or a sick child. They wanted to tell their stories. They wanted to share their experiences so that other mothers would feel less alone.

So, I created a website and a blog. Here, I shared the photos from the Mother's Day sessions and started connecting women through their stories about this sacred, common ground of motherhood. Every day on the Good Mother Project blog, another mama gets to tell her truth. She gets to see her beauty and strength reflected back through her own words, and through the comments and support of the other women who read her story.

I thought my *Eat Pray Love* journey started on that kitchen floor and ended in Bordeaux. But it is so far from over. Sometimes, I think it's just beginning.

Penny Prayers

Aimee Halfpenny

I t was the summer of 2010, and my unworn wedding dress
was in the backseat of my Volvo. I had been driving around
with it for two weeks. The dress rode with me to work, to the
grocery store, to Zumba. It was a silent passenger I couldn't
bring myself to get rid of.

I first read *Eat Pray Love* in 2007. I came to it hesitantly. I
distinctly remember seeing the book displayed in stores and dis-
missing it. Another story about someone who figured it all out,
magically got her happy ending, and would tell me what to do in
just five easy steps? No thank you. But a friend confessed she
thought of me when the author described her depression. Intrigued, I bought the book.

I found, to my surprise, that I related to this broken woman
who was desperately uncomfortable in her own skin. Like her,
my thirst for travel was intense and I understood the need to run
through fields and explore ruins. I had reforested hills in Oa-

xaca and worked with the rural poor in Nicaragua. My world cracked open, and I received far more from the beautiful souls I met on my adventures than they ever did from me. They taught me that the act of giving isn't a by-product of material wealth, it's a way of life and a daily practice.

So I plowed through Italy and India and then something happened—I got stuck. I was stuck for about three years. I'm not completely sure why I couldn't continue, but my best guess is this: the heart cannot absorb what it's not ready for.

It wasn't until I was suffering through my broken engagement, driving around with that dress in my car and feeling like my spirit had been pushed off a cliff that I returned to *Eat Pray Love*. This time, I took it in like a rescued fledgling being fed by an eyedropper. My entire life, I had wanted to be chosen. And then I was. And then I wasn't. My fiancé changed his mind three months before our wedding, and the very public nature of calling it off meant everyone—all the people I loved and the cake baker besides—now knew what I suspected my whole life: I was unlovable.

I needed the rest of Liz's story. It was time to get out of India and make my passage to Bali.

The engagement had ended dramatically, but the process of severing the relationship was slow.

I finished the book and, as if divinely scheduled, the movie of *Eat Pray Love* hit theaters ten days after my ex and I finally called it quits. I wept through the entire film. Shortly thereafter I made a trip to Sedona, Arizona. I spent my days climbing red rocks in the sun. I visited the Chapel of the Holy Cross, an architectural masterpiece built into the side of a hill. In a daze, I made my way around the chapel's gift shop, full of books and trinkets.

I came across a display of medals of patron saints and started picking up different ones, pressing their raised surfaces against my thumb. I wondered if these icons could actually deliver peace.

The last one I held was "Divine Mercy." Yes, this is the one, I thought. I hung it around my neck, believing it would stay there indefinitely.

W hen I was fifteen, I fell in love with Ireland. I think it was those bookstore calendars, all the mossy castles and rolling hills. Then I discovered there was a Halfpenny Bridge in Dublin, and that cemented it. This was clearly my land; these were my people. I decided that before I was married I would go to Ireland and stand as a Halfpenny on the Halfpenny Bridge.

I took my self-proclaimed spiritual pilgrimage very seriously and boasted to others about it. The thing is, I really did feel as if part of my heart was waiting for me on that bridge, and I had to travel to Ireland if I ever wanted to claim it.

Eat Pray Love resurrected that old dream of mine. It occurred to me that I would have been married without ever standing on that bridge. Maybe it was a sign. Maybe that piece of my heart was still there, still waiting for me. Maybe the person I was meant to choose was myself.

My teenage promise became a call to action. I had to get to Ireland—and I was hell-bent on going alone. Even so, it took a village to get me there. I was dirt-poor, working for a nonprofit where I had been in a salary freeze for eighteen months. Supportive friends stepped up, offering rides, travel guides and advice. My best friend, Kelli, loaned me the money for my plane ticket until my tax return came and I could pay her back. I told her, somewhat waveringly, of my plan. We cried together in her bathroom, and she whispered, "You have to do this, Aimee. You have to."

I arrived in Dublin on an unusually warm day in late February. I wandered the city taking in the Georgian architecture and trying to understand the heavy Irish accents. I visited Dublin Castle and the Chester Beatty Library, which houses some of the world's rarest and earliest religious texts. Finally, after settling into my apartment, I knew it was time. I looked out over the rooftops and took a deep breath. I asked God to make me brave, and the tiny voice inside me said, "Be present. That's what I want for you in this, to be present."

Having a peaceful or meaningful moment on the Halfpenny Bridge, it turns out, is a little like finding Zen in the Lincoln Tunnel. The bridge connects a bustling business district of Dublin to the pub mecca of Temple Bar and is always packed with people. I made my way through the crowd and then I was finally doing it—I was really standing there, a Halfpenny on the Halfpenny Bridge. I asked a passing man to take a picture of me and smiled joyfully. I brought two pennies with me to cast over the side. Penny prayers. One of gratitude and one of hope.

I spent the next two weeks traveling around the country. The first week was mostly occupied with resting, reading and sobbing, and the second with dancing all night to "Galway Girl" and drinking pints of Guinness. I visited castles and cliffs and watched rugby, slipped into churches and walked cities.

My last night in Ireland, in a pub in Galway, I met a young man who toured me around his city, showing me the Spanish Arch and ushering me into Irish music sessions. We talked about life, love and heartbreak. We talked about what it meant to be *strong*, which I was labeled ad nauseam during the collapse of my engagement. I told him I was not strong—in fact, I was full of fear and still processing my loss. What's more, I would have married a man I shouldn't have. I showed him the saint medal I had purchased in Sedona, still around my neck, and shared that I wore it to get me through.

At the end of the night, before we parted ways, he said, "I have a gift for you." I was taken aback—a present for me? The kindness of this stranger surprised me.

He handed me a small medal of Saint Patrick. It seemed like a gift from God. I slipped it on and removed my Divine Mercy medal, thanking it for its service and acknowledging that someday I might need it again.

I wear Saint Patrick now as a symbol of a new time in my life. One of hope, one of peace and, for the first time, one of Halfpenny.

Road Map

——

Alexandria Hodge

I first read *Eat Pray Love* as a teenager, and still think back to it almost daily. At nineteen years old, it was shocking for me to read about a woman ending a marriage simply because she wasn't happy. My mother hadn't been happy a single day of her nearly three-decade-long marriage to my father and yet they were still together. She believed that success, happiness (despite her personal experience) and wholeness began with an intact family unit—which, of course, meant an intact marriage. And Elizabeth Gilbert hadn't only left her marriage—she had gone overseas, which was a dream of mine. And she had done this just because she wanted to; just because she thought it would heal her!

Eventually, after many tumultuous years in which we found ourselves unsuccessful in many ways, deeply unhappy and far from whole, my parents' marriage finally fell apart, no matter my mother's steadfast beliefs. I was left feeling like the casualty of it all, with a deeply entrenched cynicism about marriage, a conviction that love, in the end, was doomed to unhappiness and a prevailing uncertainty over what happiness in a relationship even looked like or who had the right to it in the first place.

After the divorce, I looked at *Eat Pray Love* in a new light. It helped me rewire what my parents had unknowingly taught me about love and marriage just when I needed those lessons most. It became my road map, a way to avoid the minefield of what I saw as my parents' mistakes.

Because of *Eat Pray Love*, I was careful about the parameters of any relationships I entered into and made sure to monitor my own happiness. Like Elizabeth, I realized that I have a right to my own well-being. I'm now in a healthy relationship with someone who is a true partner. We've made a commitment always to do the things that heal us and make us happy as individuals and as a couple. Right now, that's in the form of traveling. I just started my master's degree at University College London, and my partner is continuing his own education while we're here. Turns out love doesn't have to be unhappy after all. Thanks for the powerful life lesson, Liz.

Curing the Incurable

Amy B. Scher

When the best medical doctors in America gave up on me at the end of 2007, I was twenty-eight years old and felt the steel doors of possibility slam shut. All the hope I'd been mustering to recover from late-stage Lyme disease and its life-threatening complications had finally drained from me like water from a cracked bucket. But shortly after the last doctor delivered the last words of defeat, a new opportunity blew those doors wide open. I was accepted into an experimental stem cell treatment program in a tiny clinic in Delhi, India.

India!

Having read *Eat Pray Love* along with the rest of the world, I had already smelled each smell with Elizabeth, tasted each taste and become enchanted by the exotic country of India. *Eat Pray Love* entertained me, allowing me to escape my own impossible life. Now, it would help me find the courage to try to save it.

At first, I was terrified of going. My doctors were against it, and I had no idea if this radical treatment would kill me or cure me. This was quite literally a last-ditch effort as there were no other options left. Then I thought of Elizabeth's colorful stories and transformed them into a landscape for what could be my own crazy adventure. Before *Eat Pray Love*, I knew almost nothing about India. But Liz's own bravery made accessible the idea of a woman traveling alone to a country like India. It wasn't yet popular, but it was definitely possible. On December 9, 2007, I boarded a plane for New Delhi.

How I Ate

Why oh why can't this be in China? That was my honest-to-goodness first thought about the location of this new treatment. I was dying, and all I wanted was Chinese food! In fact, there was no food on earth I disliked more than Indian food. My first meals at the hospital were saucy, earth-toned globs that had "no name, ma'am" when I asked what they were.

The wafting smells, the pungent taste and the mixed textures of curry were too much for my delicate digestion. Often unable to keep any food down at all, I worried about the consequences for my already underweight body.

At about the three-week mark of my stay, though, something happened. The smells that used to nauseate me started to feel like a comfort. I began having cravings for my favorite "green chicken," delighting the hospital cook to no end. I started to embrace mutton and ghee and all the foods I had resisted. My body started to long for each plate, and sometimes I asked for seconds and even thirds.

By the time I returned home, I had a new favorite cuisine and an extra twenty pounds of healthy body weight to show for it.

How I Prayed

During my first few days in India, my doctor sent a colleague of hers from another hospital to visit me. She arrived one afternoon during my nap, explaining little about who she was or what she was doing. She carried a huge purse, had long silky hair and wore intricately patterned Indian attire. She felt closer to a presence than a person. She was a perfect swirly blend of intellect and spirit, all wrapped in a sari.

As she sat with me, she began speaking of her Buddhist practice called *daimoku*—chanting with specific words that reveal one's state of inner Buddhahood. She told me the story of how several years earlier it had brought her husband back to life. I took a deep interest in Dr. M.'s practice and became her student. She invited me to her home, and as we chanted, I felt the energy shift around me and a palpable change in my own body.

Her gift became my new ritual. I fell asleep every single night staring at the bright blue wall in my hospital room and chanting, the day fading with each repetition.

How I Loved

The physiotherapy room was adorned with yellow curtains and always filled with music that was much too loud for my taste. That's where I saw her—thick, dark, curly hair hiding under a baseball hat and a giant smile that opened up to the world. Charlotte had come to visit her mother who was being treated at the hospital for amyotrophic lateral sclerosis (ALS). ALS is a fatal disease involving the nerve cells and has a life expectancy of two to five years from the time of diagnosis.

My meeting with Charlotte was never supposed to happen. I was set to return home three days earlier, but a bout of food poisoning left me unable to fly. Charlotte arrived from London to visit her mom a few days before my rescheduled flight home. For days, we laughed together almost nonstop while silently wondering what would become of our quick bonding and seemingly mystical meeting. I had never been in a relationship with a woman, but I quickly knew this could be something more than friendship. Soon we had to separate. Over the coming weeks, we wrote enough e-mails to each other to fill books. Then, three months after leaving Delhi, we decided to take the next step and meet halfway between her home in London and mine in California. We settled on Boston. The night we arrived, after our first kiss, I asked Charlotte to marry me. She said no. We laughed, and time moved on.

We racked up travel miles just to be together for a week or two at a time. Moving was impossible—her mother's health was rapidly declining, as was my father's in California. But we made it work. My dad always told me the way you know if someone is "the one" is when you feel like "it's you and me against the world, baby." And I did.

Our love story continued, but not in the typical way. We held hands over Charlotte's mother's hospital bed as she took her last breaths. We then held my dad's ashes in those same hands not long after.

While it has not all been a fairy tale, we have always remained absorbed in the magic. That feeling the first day in the physio room; the knowing we were meant to be together; the laughter and joy we find in each every day; and the absolute blessing of what we commonly refer to as "the best love story ever"—not because it's been perfect but because it's ours.

Since the day I took that giant leap of faith and gave an echoing yes! to my Indian adventure, I have survived what doctors said I never would. I have taken my healing to new heights. I have turned inward to recover completely, far beyond what medicine or stem cells or doctors could offer. I have lived, and I have lived well.

I n the years since the incurable cure, I have made up for lost time. Charlotte and I have traveled all over the world. We've eaten copious amounts of pasta in Venice, Italy, and cuddled up in a jeep while roaring over the red dirt of the South African desert.

Eat Pray Love started for me as many books do but became so much more.

Eat Pray Love gave me the chutzpah to jump into the ultimate unknowing. It gave me the courage to make it through each day in India when I only had wipes for showers, and the curiosity to take responsibility for changing my health and my life. *Eat Pray Love* helped me turn a whole lotta faith over to the Universe. Most of all, it gave me the everlasting grace to stumble and sometimes even fall, knowing that it's much more fun if you always play life like one hell of a grand adventure.

Failure to Freedom

——

Linsi Broom

M y first encounter with *Eat Pray Love* was the movie. I remember watching it and thinking that an adventure like that could never be possible for someone like me: middle-class, wrought with student loan debt, juggling a full-time job and full-time school. I couldn't imagine a world where one could just drop out of one's own life. After all, my family taught me that my name was all I had and I must—above all else—make sure that name signified responsibility, practicality and a dogged work ethic. It wasn't until 2013, when I experienced a series of very intense sudden failures—in school, in love and in life—that I began to question everything I thought I knew about what I should and should not be. About what *responsible* and *practical* even meant.

After that string of failures, I moved across the country, desperate to start over and rebuild my life. I wanted to replace all

that I had lost, and quickly. But I kept failing—in fact, for someone who had never failed at anything (until I failed at everything), it felt like I was overdosing on it.

During this time, I happened to meet an intrepid British
traveler who was making his way across America on six dollars a
day. We became fast friends, and as he shared stories of his experiences, something stirred inside me. Here was this regular
guy doing something completely unexpected. He was taking a
risk, and he was being rewarded with human connection, cosmic
support and adventure. I returned to the internal argument I
had when I first watched *Eat Pray Love.* Could I do that? Could
I have an adventure for the pure sake of personal growth?

I let those questions marinate. I found a temporary job, and
I started putting money away—subconsciously at first, but then
intentionally. I started imagining the trip I would take. I had
traveled internationally before but never alone and never anywhere exotic. At night after work, I would research places and
dream of the possibilities. One day during a conversation with a
coworker, she mentioned how one of her lifelong goals was to do
a Vipassana course in Nepal. Even though I taught yoga and
meditated, I was unfamiliar with Vipassana and only had a vague
idea of where Nepal was located. As I listened to her, something
clicked inside of me. I just knew. That's what I would do! I would
go to Nepal and take a Vipassana course. Later that day, I applied for the course. I told people, "Oh, I'm sure I won't get accepted." A few days later, I received my acceptance e-mail. My
temporary job was ending in a few months. All of my colleagues
were making other arrangements—finding new jobs, starting
new ventures. Anytime someone asked me what my plans were,

I would say, "Oh, I'm not sure. Maybe I'll travel." And then I would laugh nervously. I knew that I was going on the trip, but I was afraid to say it out loud for fear of judgment.

In my private time, I would fret over the details. Did I have enough money? What would my family and friends think? Was I being foolish? I gave myself ultimatums. If I found a job before my departure date, then I would cancel the trip. Still, I kept planning. I decided that I would start in Thailand, make my way to Nepal for the course and then let the momentum of the trip lead me where it might. I would return to the States after three months (approximately how long I thought my budget would last).

Finally, after months of self-doubt and procrastination, I made the final leap and bought my plane ticket. It was done. I was going.

Having my ticket in hand didn't stop me from continuing to agonize over my decision. Even on the plane, I felt sick to my stomach. But once my feet were on the ground in Thailand, I was committed. I joked after I left Thailand for Nepal, "That was certainly the 'Eat' portion of my *Eat Pray Love* adventure." And on the plane to Nepal, as my breath caught in my chest at the first glimpse of the Himalayas, I thought to myself, "This has to be the 'Love' part." *Eat Pray Love* found me wherever I went. People I met would kid me and ask me if I was on some kind of mission of self-discovery. I'd laugh, but I began to feel that Elizabeth Gilbert and I were cosmically connected—as single women, as brave souls, as truth seekers. And then, through a series of unforeseen events, I ended up on the island of Bali. I had forgotten that Bali was where Elizabeth, too, had ended her journey, until late one night when I was having dinner at a local *warung*. I was chatting with a Balinese man about my trip, and he said, "You remind me of that woman who came here and wrote that book."

That night, as I was getting ready for bed, I glanced at the bookshelf in my guesthouse and literally laughed out loud. There on the shelf sat a weathered copy of, yes, *Eat Pray Love*. I had only ever seen the movie; now, over the next few days, I devoured the book. I related to all of Elizabeth's stories about meditation, having just spent ten days in silence myself, and especially the deep longing she felt for connection and understanding. Tears streamed down my face as I reached the end of the book. My own trip was coming to a close and there was no fairy-tale ending in sight. I was still very much alone.

On my last evening in Bali, I sat on a cliff overlooking the ocean. As the sun faded out of sight, I thought to myself, "I took a chance. I went against everything I thought I should be. I have seen and experienced love in every way possible. I am okay. I am more than okay—I am content."

All those years ago, *Eat Pray Love* sparked a question in my mind: Could I do something "irresponsible"; could I take a risk with no guarantees?

Finally, I had my answer: I could. I could question the narrative I had been taught about myself. I could take a risk and have it pay off in dividends. I will be forever changed by that trip and the people I met along the way. Thank you, Elizabeth, from the bottom of my heart.

Steps

—

Melissa Bergstrom

I discovered *Eat Pray Love* in the fall of 2009. At only twenty-six years old, I had just left my job on disability. I had been suffering from debilitating back pain on and off for nearly two years, and that October it became unbearable. One afternoon I left work, simply unable to sit at my desk any longer. The next day I called in sick and lay in bed all day. I did the same thing the following day, and the day after that. I never returned to work.

I was also taking time off from a small all-female theater company I founded. Truth be told, I was okay not working as an office manager anymore, but as someone who had always considered acting one of the great loves of her life, it hurt me so much to drop out of the theater.

My life had become incredibly isolated. Going hiking or out to dinner with my fiancé or even to family gatherings was now all things of the past. I questioned whether I was even going to be able to walk down the aisle at my wedding.

This was not the life I had imagined for myself. Would I be bedridden forever? Would I ever be able to hang out with friends again? Would I be able to act? I felt crushed underneath the weight of my physical pain and mental anguish. It was like having a huge rock on my chest that made it impossible to breathe.

Since I was spending most of my days on the floor, reading became an easy way to pass the time. I've always been a passionate reader, devouring book after book. As a kid, I would stay up way past my bedtime, reading by flashlight under the covers, feeling like the book in my hand was performing alchemy.

Books were my time machine. I flew a fighter plane with Hannah Senesh in World War II, danced with Romeo and Juliet at the Capulets' ball, sat quietly with Anne Frank in her annex. This time, I hoped reading would work its magic in a new kind of way, distracting me from the pain and perhaps delivering me from disability altogether.

It didn't.

I read books on healing back pain, books on stretching and more books on diet and mindfulness. Nothing helped. One afternoon when my soon-to-be mother-in-law was visiting me, as she often did, she said, "You know, Melissa. I know you want to find a cure for this. But I'm worried that you're not doing anything but thinking and reading and worrying about your pain. Maybe you should read some other kind of book, something different." She gave me a well-read copy of *Eat Pray Love* that she had recently finished and said, "I think you will LOVE this."

I had seen the book in bookstores and knew that it was a bestseller. For some reason, the idea that a book was loved by the masses made me wonder if I would be able to connect to it on a deeper level. If a book had been read by millions of people all over the world, would it feel personal enough to me?

Despite my initial hesitation, I dove in, and from the first page I could understand why my mother-in-law connected to the story so much. I felt like Liz was writing a letter just to me. I suddenly felt like I had a new friend who, yes, also cried on her bathroom floor but was also funny and fierce and adventurous. Her life had been a complete, seemingly inescapable mess, and yet here she was eating pizza, meditating and living!

With every page I read, I felt less trapped in my body. My imagination, which has always been one of my favorite parts of myself, broke open and I felt freer than I had in months. It was as if Liz had put her hand on my shoulder and said, "I know you are going through hell right now. I've been here. But I've also walked the road out, one step at a time."

I was still in pain, but there had to be steps I could take, even from my own apartment.

I started to meditate—not a lot, and nothing earth-shattering occurred during these brief sessions, but after having felt robbed of my body for so long, I loved being able to take control over something as simple as breath.

After that, I started paying attention to the food that I ate. Even in pain, I still had my robust appetite, and I began to be grateful for being hungry and having access to fresh, healthy foods. Meals became a pleasure. Inspired by the part of the book where Liz eats hard-boiled eggs in her flat in Rome and reads the newspaper, I began to relish eating rich buttery toast, chocolate gelato and takeout from my favorite Greek restaurant.

I wasn't well enough to go to the theater to see plays, but I discovered Netflix had versions of some of my favorite productions, along with classics I had never seen. I watched these from the comfort of my bed, with my cat curled by my side. Life looked just a little less awful.

I decided to start taking daily walks, five minutes or less, in the parking lot of my apartment complex. It wasn't the beach of Bali, but after months of being inside for days at a time, it looked new to me. I noticed cats in windows, passed by dogs out for their daily walks and heard birds. I felt sunshine. I began to feel joy and hope, to notice beauty. There were still plenty of things to experience and to love in this world.

It took six more months for my back pain to disappear, and almost a dozen doctors, daily workouts at the gym, stretching at home and a lot of loving myself through it all. Liz showed me that we cannot heal without loving our whole selves, and that it takes courage to imagine we can get better. I returned the copy of *Eat Pray Love* to my mother-in-law but imagined that its lessons had seeped into me, never to be lost.

I was able to walk down the aisle at my wedding, and I tore it up on the dance floor. As I danced with my whole body to my favorite music, it felt like coming home to my authentic self. I moved to Boston to attend grad school for theater and met people who have made my life so much richer. I traveled and founded a second theater company with one of my oldest and dearest friends. *Eat Pray Love* is inextricably linked to all these things—it came to me at a time when I needed it most and further proved to me how powerful it is for one person to share his or her story. The book was a gift I'll spend the rest of my life giving back. Now I'm working on writing my own story, and I hope that in sharing it, I might give that gift to someone else. I'll make the *Eat Pray Love* circle complete.

A Bonk on the Head

Kahla Kiker

God didn't speak to me the way he did to Elizabeth Gilbert in *Eat Pray Love*, and it was the floor of my closet, not my bathroom, that I found myself curled up on for the thousandth time, lights off and tears streaming down my cheeks as I hoped for just a few minutes of peace.

Work had been even more difficult than usual that day, and I didn't want to take my frustrations out on my family. I was good at my job and had plenty of experience, but no college degree, so I was belittled constantly. The atmosphere was toxic, and I was making myself physically ill with stress. I knew I needed to quit my job, but the bills were getting paid and food was on the table, and I felt guilty for even thinking about doing something so selfish.

My husband was working late again, the laundry was piled up all over the house and my children were screaming at one another. As I sat on the floor of my closet, all I could think was:

This is not my life.
I felt completely and utterly alone.

Three weeks later, when I was on the verge of severe depression, a coworker came into my office and said she was leaving the company. She was moving to Argentina for a three-month sabbatical inspired by this book she had just read, *Eat Pray Love.* I was shocked. I was happy for her, but also envious and sad. I wanted to run away and find myself, too, but I couldn't. I left my office in tears and spent my lunch break at my local bookstore, on a mission to find this magical, seemingly transformative book—and find it I did.

I started reading the first few pages right there in the bookstore and immediately felt something that I hadn't in a long time—hope. I dialed my boss from the bookstore and told him I was sick and wouldn't be returning to work that day. Then I went home and began reading for real. I devoured *Eat Pray Love* in one sitting. I remember having to take a few deep breaths, exhausted, before I finally fell asleep. The next morning, I woke up feeling the energy of possibility. Even though my boss angrily commented on the previous day's absence, I didn't let it bother me. Instead, I just smiled to myself—I was going to enroll in college! I was taking charge of my future while also giving my boss a metaphorical middle finger. It felt fantastic.

The journey was harder than I could have known, but every late night and bout of tears were worth it as I walked across the stage to receive my degree, and again, when I found an even better job where I felt truly appreciated.

I was content with my life—for a while. Then my brother

passed away, and I began to feel a void creeping in. I looked at my children as they grew older, my husband as he moved up in his company, and felt sure that everything in my life was evolving—except for me. I thought about my brother's short life and began to question my life's purpose outside of being a mother, employee and wife. I was losing myself again.

I spent three years struggling with depression, trying to find something that would ease the hole in my heart. Until the day I turned thirty-six—the very age my brother was when he died. That day, I decided I needed to clear the negative energy in my house, starting with all the clutter that had accumulated in my closet. I was pulling boots down from the upper shelves when I was struck on the head by a book. Yes, you guessed it—*Eat Pray Love*! I had recently begun trying to cultivate a more intentional, spiritual way of being while dealing with my grief, so I felt sure this moment was trying to tell me something.

I listened—I sat down and read the book again. But this time I wasn't trying to escape anything. This time, I was looking for love—for myself, and for my creativity.

When I was completing my college degree, I discovered how much I truly enjoyed writing. I was one of the few students who actually looked forward to writing papers, and I did well on them. I felt like stories and characters could spill out of me at any moment. And yet, as happy as writing made me, once I graduated, it soon became a distant memory, displaced by work and family obligations.

It took that bonk on the head for me to finally start writing again—this time, for no one but myself. Initially it was therapy, a way to deal with my grief. Then it became entertainment and stress relief—a creative outlet at the end of a tough workday.

Finally, my writing turned into an exploration of curiosity, of "what if?" And then, I really did it—one year ago, I hit "publish" on my first book.

I still find myself in my closet each week, but now I'm there by choice, grabbing a few minutes of silence to recharge and re-balance the energies of the day.

So much has changed since the afternoon I fled to the bookstore determined to find *Eat Pray Love*—and again since it bonked me on the head. Now, as I look around at the successful, fulfilling life I've created, I can happily say *Eat Pray Love* made me do it.

Someone Like Me

———

Sandra Roussy

L ike a lot of other women in my circle of friends and across the globe, ten years ago I read *Eat Pray Love* in a ferocious, envious way. Within the first few pages I was engulfed. Within the first few chapters I knew.

I knew that my life was at a standstill; that it lacked passion and purpose. I also knew that something had to change. I was successful at what many thought of as a "creative" career; I had a healthy daughter; I owned my own home and paid my own bills. But in reality, my career took up most of my time and energy, time and energy I wanted to spend on my own creative pursuits; ten years ago my now-grown-up daughter was in day care and then home alone eating frozen pizza more times than I wanted to admit; the house belonged to the bank; and the bills often got paid late or on credit. How did I get here?

I knew that change was possible because someone like me had already done it. She had picked herself up off the floor and stepped out of her comfort zone, determined to discover who she really was and what she wanted. One day, couldn't I do that, too? Couldn't "someone like me" become "me"?

I wanted to see the world while volunteering and working; I desperately wanted to make a difference with people and with the environment. For years, though, I procrastinated, making excuses as to why I couldn't move forward. "One day" was always the next day. Change felt impossible. I was paralyzed by fear and what ifs. What if I risk too much and fail? What if I make a huge mistake? What if I get my wallet stolen on the first day in a new country? What if it's really humid and I can't keep my bangs straight? I feared fear, and I feared myself.

So I faded into a socially acceptable routine that made me more and more miserable. Made me so miserable, in fact, that all those years I wasn't moving forward, I was numbing myself with a lot of wine. It was good company, until, of course, it wasn't, and then I was just waiting to hit rock bottom. I didn't know what that would look like, exactly, but I figured when I hit it I would know. So I carried on, waiting to crash. And then, I got tired of waiting. I decided that rock bottom didn't really exist—it was only an excuse to stay on a path of self-destruction without taking any responsibility for it. But I knew if I stopped, all my failures would smack me right in the face. I wasn't ready for that.

Then 2014 came careening in.

It was an early February morning, my mother's birthday.

I called to wish her happy birthday, and she told me they'd found a mass on my dad's pancreas. He was going for more tests.

The drive to work was a blur. The minute I got to the office, I Googled everything I could about the pancreas. My dad was dying. I was trying to process this information and keep my composure when I was called into the president's office. I was told the company was struggling, thanked for my excellent service and let go. Was this day really happening?

The next eight months were spent caring for my ailing father. I was actually secretly thankful my boss let me go, because it gave me the time to be with my dad. I was there with him as much as possible, through the bad, the scary and the really ugly. I watched him fade away into a shell of what he used to be, and then I lost him completely. I could have never imagined the intense pain that comes with losing a person you are so deeply bonded to. The pain jolted me awake, and I refused to numb it this time.

I was jobless and fatherless. Now, what would I do?

I thought of *Eat Pray Love*, and my fear faded away. I had romanticized Liz's story for so long, thinking it was unattainable for someone like me. But it wasn't. Life is so short—my father's death made that clear—and I didn't want to leave it with regrets in my heart.

I decided to finally set off on my own journey. I sold my house and got rid of everything that wasn't necessary and therefore would be weighing me down. I felt so light and free! I would make my own decisions, and for the first time know that those decisions weren't being dictated by societal standards or a desire to please. I wasn't going to merely step out of my comfort zone—I was going to leap thousands of miles away from it. There would be no turning back. It felt right.

In autumn 2015, I headed off to the magnificent Galápagos Islands in Ecuador, to study and volunteer. I've always been fascinated by the theory of evolution; how it's constantly in action, shaping our own existence. What better place to be, then, than with Darwin's finches, which started it all? And from there, I'll let life take me where it may, trusting that where I am and what I'm doing is serving a creative purpose and is beneficial to myself, to others and, most of all, to this beautiful planet. My daughter has become my biggest supporter as I embark on this new chapter, and I'm proud to show her that anything is possible, at any age.

Eat Pray Love made me believe I could do it. Fearlessly, onward bound.

Pepperoni Epiphanies

—

James Belmont

I would love to say that *Eat Pray Love* made me jump on the first plane to some exotic destination, eat amazing food, find God and fall in love with a perfectly imperfect man. In fact, as I get older, that might be the story I'll tell (and who's going to argue with an old curmudgeon like I'll be?).

Until then, though, this is what really happened.

I closed the book and just sat there. I was dumbfounded. I actually felt kind of abandoned. Liz had left me! My lifeline to her was cut off as she rode into the sunset. And not only had she left me, but she had left me with questions, and with not one freaking slice of life-altering margarita pizza! What was I supposed to do?

I would like to say that I then progressed, with decorum and grace, of course, through the stages of grief and loss, before arriving at acceptance. Again, in my sunset years, this is how I'm going to tell this story.

Instead, I bawled my eyes out and then grew very angry. There had to be more, right? More love, more wisdom, more food sent straight from the gods! But there was nothing: just me. I was all I had at that moment, and that had to be enough.

In *Eat Pray Love*, Liz started her healing by talking to God and eventually found out (in a good way) that she was also talking to herself. Well, God and I already talked. Like, a lot.

Okay, I'll be honest; I did most of the talking and not a lot of listening. I figured by now She must be sick of my prattle.

So I started actually talking to myself. For two days, every moment when I wasn't working, I was at home having the peace summit of my life.

At first it felt somewhat the same as when I talked to God, except this time, there was a really judgmental asshole on the other end of the conversation. He was super critical sometimes, and super stubborn for most of it. As our conversations grew longer and more intense, I came to an unpleasant realization: he HATED me, more than I ever thought possible.

Slowly, over these two nights of hanging out (with pizza) with that prick, I began to stop talking and start listening to what he was saying. I saw through his bravado. He saw through my fear. I saw through his promiscuity; he acknowledged my past pain. He acknowledged my loneliness but showed me that I was not alone. I started to show him that forgiving both of us was probably the only path we could follow. That scared him. He wasn't sure he could do that.

I confronted him about why he hated me so much. He responded that I didn't deserve to be loved or have any of the blessings I had.

I was shocked and confused. I didn't think I was really all

that blessed. He pointed out all the blessings I had in work, friends, family and (he admitted begrudgingly) talents. I asked him why I didn't deserve them.

"I know what darkness lies in there, dude!" he snapped over a mouthful of pizza. "The thoughts you will never admit; the unbridled selfishness and the sense of superiority. Are you trying to convince me that you deserve to be loved?"

I was stunned. I had no idea he felt this way. (To be honest, I was also a bit stunned that I had just dude-ed myself.)

"But—I love," I responded, weakly at first.

"Really?" came the snarky reply.

"Yes, I do. It might be quiet, or it might be loud, but I LOVE!"

I am not sure which one of us was more surprised that I was shouting.

"I love," I continued, much quieter. "I have the capacity to love. We both know what it's like to lose that for a while, and I will celebrate that fact. It's a rare and precious gift to love, and it should be shared. I've lost it before, and I will not lose it again. And I will no longer fear loving myself the way I love other people. Is that clear?"

He got quiet for a moment.

"You know I'm never leaving you," he stated, almost saddened by the fact.

"I know," I replied. "And to be frank, I need you. You are a part of me. I acknowledge that. But you are not the only part, and, to be honest, not even a majority shareholder anymore."

My living room got really quiet. The sounds of a YouTube video could be faintly heard as I just stood there, staring, with a dripping slice of pepperoni pizza in my hand.

A lot of questions went through my mind.

Did I just put a major dent into my epic level of self-loathing?

Is my pizza getting cold?

Why am I thinking of a lion?

Did the neighbors hear all that?

The eerie thing was, this all seemed so familiar to me. Where had I heard a conversation like this before? I was so worked up, I couldn't remember. And why was I still thinking of a lion?

I looked down, and there was Liz on my coffee table—well, her book anyway—partially covered by the pizza box from two nights ago. I had gotten so worked up during my conversation that I forgot I was mad at her for leaving me.

I opened the book to a dog-eared page. And this is what it roared: YOU HAVE NO IDEA HOW STRONG MY LOVE IS!!!!!!!!!

The chattering, negative thoughts in my mind scattered in the wind of this statement like birds and jackrabbits and antelopes. They hightailed it out of there, terrified.

I had found my lion. Cowardly, friendly, but all mine. In me.

My adventure of the past two days was over. I had made a stand against self-loathing and began loving myself for all of who I was. Even as this chapter closed, though, I realized that a new, more fulfilling adventure was only just beginning: learning how to live with myself.

The List

—

Annmarie Kostyk

I'm not worthy.

I wasn't raised to be independent. I was raised to look for someone wealthy to take care of me. After all, it was just as easy to fall in love with a rich man as it was a poor man. To me, though, money didn't matter. I just wanted someone who loved me unconditionally and made me laugh.

As a child, I was plagued by asthma and allergies, and constantly told I couldn't be like the other kids, couldn't do what they did. I was alternately overprotected and overexposed to allergens—smoke, pets, Christmas trees—that made my condition unbearable. Many nights I prayed that I would not die. At five years old, I was bargaining with God for my life. I was afraid.

My fear was only exacerbated by twelve years of Catholic school. I didn't understand this religion that claimed to be superior over all others. Why was my religion right and others wrong? I was constantly afraid of making a mistake or breaking one of the many rules drilled into us from an early age. I was afraid of not going to church; I was afraid of birth control and afraid of getting pregnant. I worried that if I didn't do what I was told, didn't do the things that were expected of me, I would be denied all the good things in life. I would be punished.

My mother expected me to be a doctor so I spent my entire high school career taking science and math classes. Yet I dreamed of traveling the globe and working in an art museum. Unsurprisingly, I hated school and began to believe I couldn't do anything well. Then I sabotaged myself so that belief became reality. I felt self-conscious around other kids, like I couldn't connect to them, and I had no idea who I was or who I was becoming. All I knew was that I was unhappy.

When I went away to college, I found freedom for the first time in my life. I also found alcohol, which became a coping mechanism for me. I didn't know how to fit in and was desperate to do so. I drank heavily socially on and off for about a decade. Eventually, I developed a sensitivity to alcohol and almost died. Once I stopped drinking, I began having panic attacks. They'd happen when I was stuck in traffic or out walking alone. I went on antidepressants. I had no social life, since venturing outside could mean another panic attack. The world seemed unreachable to me.

Ten years ago, I saw Elizabeth Gilbert on *Oprah*. I was forty years old and still living with my parents. I had never married. I didn't have a boyfriend, children or any real social life. I also had never heard of *Eat Pray Love*. Yet listening to Ms. Gilbert tell her story, I felt such a connection with her that I cried a few times during the show. Realizing that she had tried to be everything everyone else wanted and expected her to be, even though she wanted none of those things—that hit me right in the heart. The fact that she needed a journey to find herself resonated in my soul; it felt decadent to me. I wanted that, too.

I went out and purchased the book, and read it in one sitting. I highlighted. I wrote in the margins, something I never do. I cried so many times, I thought I was losing it. When I finished, I put the book down and let out a huge sigh. My life could be fixed. I could feel whole again. I just needed to find what worked for me. What was my *Eat Pray Love?*

I made a very long list of things I wanted to do or try, and things I wanted to change about my life. I knew tackling the list would be a long, ongoing task, and that was okay. It took me forty years to end up in this position, so it made sense that it would take a long time to become who I wanted to be: a loving person who is constantly evolving, growing and experiencing new things.

Two of the top items on my list were, of course, meditation and yoga. I went to the library and researched meditation. I borrowed books about spirituality, Hinduism, Buddhism and self-help.

I started meditating daily. It was tough at first, but I asked the universe to be patient with me since I really needed this. I needed to feel grounded, centered and at peace. I did the work, and the universe answered. Slowly, I built up my practice from five minutes to thirty minutes. I felt great afterward. I was calm. I started sleeping well. I moved out of my parents' home.

I signed up for a beginner's yoga class. After my first lesson, I cried. My instructor told me that often happens, because yoga releases emotions. She was happy my first class was so successful; I, on the other hand, felt like crap. Still, I kept going. Now, when I do yoga, I feel like I'm reaching my soul.

Over the past ten years, I have been doing exactly what I set out to do. I'm evolving as a being in this wonderful universe. I've learned that I can take care of myself. And I can take care of that kid who, I realize, wasn't all that sick to begin with. I nurture that kid. On occasion, I color. (Yes, I bought myself colored pencils, markers and a beautiful coloring book just for adults.) I became a healthy, active woman. I have a loving circle of friends. I have work that makes me feel good. I'm not at all religious, though I discovered I am extremely spiritual. I believe in kindness and love. I am at peace. I feel lighter.

I'm fifty now. I've crossed off so many items on my list of things to do and try—but I've probably added twice as many new ones! I still have fears, obstacles and doubts, but really, who doesn't? And once or twice a year, I reread my copy of *Eat Pray Love* to remind me of my journey. I remember how far I've come, and I'm proud of myself. This in turn reminds me that I have so much more to experience and enjoy.

Thank you, Elizabeth Gilbert. Sharing your journey in *Eat Pray Love* saved me.

I am worthy.

Living Well

—

Nosipho Kota

O n December 15, 2001, I was diagnosed with HIV. I remember sitting in the consultation room afterward, completely numb. I couldn't bring myself to even stand up and leave. In the months after my diagnosis, I slipped into depression. I didn't have the courage to disclose my status to my family or friends, and instead threw myself into my work as a journalist for the *Weekend Post* in Port Elizabeth, South Africa. At night, I would lock myself in my rented room, afraid to venture outside. I was convinced that people would know I was HIV positive just by looking at me. I was afraid to laugh and afraid to have an opinion. Meaningful friendships or relationships felt impossible. I didn't think I was fit to participate in my own life. Instead, I let shame and guilt consume me. These feelings ate at the core of who I was until I became just a shadow of myself.

I suffered like this for three years, until I finally sought the help of a psychologist who offered me a different perspective on what life with HIV/AIDS could look like. She was empathetic and helped me work through my fear of getting very sick. I began to understand how the virus works on the body, and that if I ate healthily and took my medication, I could go on to live a long and meaningful life. Most important, I could watch my son grow up. I was pregnant when I discovered I was HIV positive; AZT therapy had ensured my son was delivered safely and HIV-free, and now I was determined to be present for him—to care for him and see him become the young man he is today. He is my reason for living.

Therapy helped build up my courage, and after three months I felt ready to disclose to my mother and sister. My mother was shocked but supportive. She didn't understand the intricacies of life with HIV but said she would do all she could to help. My sister lives in Johannesburg and so wasn't available for day-to-day matters but told me I could always rely on her for emotional support.

My then boyfriend, the father of my son, was a different matter. I was terrified of disclosing to him, even more so than I had been with my family, because of the stigma and blame that I feared would follow. And I was right. When I finally mustered enough courage to tell him, he rejected me. I begged and pleaded for him not to leave me; I couldn't bear to be alone. He agreed to stay, but our relationship was never the same after that. It felt like he used my HIV positive status as a reason to treat me horribly, and I took the mistreatment silently, hoping that somehow things would get better.

It was during this time that a friend recommended I read *Eat Pray Love*. I think she felt it would resonate with me because it was the story of a woman who resurrected her life from the ashes of her divorce and managed to really make something of it. I soaked Liz's words in. I realized that, like her, I had "fallen in love with the highest potential of a man, rather than with the man himself." My boyfriend was never going to be what I wanted him to be. We weren't living together; he offered neither financial nor emotional support to me and our son. I wanted better for us. I wanted my son to have integrity and to grow into a responsible young man. I knew I had to end things.

My boyfriend and I had been together for four years. Cutting ties with him was heart-wrenching but also liberating. I began nurturing myself back to spiritual and emotional health. I went on long walks and watched movies. I sought solace in books and in journaling. I made new friends. I traveled around South Africa. I started to dream again and self-published my first poetry collection. I am finding my way around loneliness. These days, I invite it in and sit with it, because I know it's a fleeting devil and soon it will pass. I am content in my own skin. When people reject me—and they do—because of my status and their ignorance, I move right along. I don't lose any sleep over it. I have faith that I will find a man who will love me regardless of my status. I know that I am beautiful, and deserving, and it does not serve me to accept anything less than a great, earthshaking, once-in-a-lifetime love.

I am living the life of my dreams as a writer and have become a source of inspiration to friends and family members who are also living with HIV. Because of me, they are able to see—as I learned myself—that one can have HIV and still live well, and with meaning. It's been fourteen years, and I've come full circle, though every day I am still learning, growing and coming into my own. My son is very proud of all that I have endured. He believes in me. He is the apple of my eye.

Thanks, Liz.

Bread and Cheese

Nicole Massaro

I tapped the button to buy the *Eat Pray Love* audiobook and left my phone on the kitchen counter while it downloaded. I knew I would need a positive distraction very soon. With a heavy heart, I walked into the next room and told my partner of five years that I was leaving for good. I'd been hoping that he would catch up with me one day and help me live out all my aspirations, but in my heart, I knew he wasn't that guy. So did he, really. We'd been best friends, inseparable for years, but that was where it ended. We cried together for a long time. Finally, I pulled out of the driveway, car already packed, and pressed Play. Liz Gilbert started talking as I began my journey to a new life in a new city, alone.

It felt like an ocean existed between my new home and everyone I had decided to leave behind. I was in a strange place with a broken heart, and, in *Eat Pray Love*, so was Liz. Listening to her tell her story meant that someone was there in spirit sharing my thoughts and feelings (and bread and cheese). By the time I finished the book, I knew great things were waiting for me if I only just reached for them.

Thanks to *Eat Pray Love*, I stopped saying no. Saying yes meant opening myself up to people and possibilities. At first, going outside my comfort zone was terrifying. My ego was bruised a time or two. Mostly, though, there was a beautiful pay-off in the form of a great new friend or a challenge to meet.

So, I learned to let myself be a beginner. I started running, eventually finishing two half marathons, and then allowed myself to stop running when I grew tired of it. I tried yoga, grew to love it, and now regularly practice in ninety-degree rooms. I kayaked (badly), camped, hiked and explored. I crocheted. I'm learning to teach English as a foreign language.

What's more, I learned to let myself be a stranger at home and abroad. I traveled to places I'd never been, jumped from bridges and swam in clear oceans. I went to parties in town where I didn't know anyone. I fell in love.

I allowed myself to indulge in things that interested me and brought me joy, instead of running in place waiting for something amazing to happen. And, wouldn't you know, while I was actually *living* my life, amazing things happened!

These days, I like to think of *Eat Pray Love* as a door that opened at just the right time, inviting and inspiring me to discover my true self. It's a journey that takes courage (and sometimes bread and cheese), and it probably never ends, but it is infinitely rewarding.

Out of the Ashes

——

Regan Spencer

E *at Pray Love* taught me how to live when I most wanted to die. It helped save my life.

A year ago, I was self-destructing, crumbling in the clutches of anorexia and addiction. To make matters worse, I was in such denial I couldn't even recognize all the ways my life was imploding. I was twenty-four and exhausted from propping up a facade that would convince myself and everyone else I was fine. I wasn't fine. Anorexia is a compulsive, addictive disorder in which you impose rigid rules about food and your body in order to feel in control, and—this is key—you cannot stop on your own.

A week before my twenty-fifth birthday, on my way to my job that I hated, that fact hit me like a brick wall: I couldn't stop my behavior. No matter how hard I tried (and I had tried); no matter how many different doctors and therapists I saw; no matter who loved me (and I had a good man, my partner of five years, waiting for me at home), I couldn't stop starving myself. What's more, I realized I had been getting high almost daily for years to ignore this fact. And I wasn't just physically starved; I could suddenly feel in my heart and soul the devastating, petrifying emptiness I had been running from.

Eat Pray Love found its way into my life just before this. I say "found its way" because I really didn't seek it out; in fact, I was avoiding it. I was cynical, rebellious and arrogant. I hated trends, and when I first heard about the book's bestseller status and movie deal, I wrote it off as a girly fad. One night at a friend's apartment, someone put the movie on. Despite my determination to hate it, Elizabeth's story spoke to something deep inside me. Her speech about being the "permeable membrane" shook me to my core. I couldn't get it out of my head. I had a sneaky feeling this book could change my life, but I was too high-and-mighty to buy it. In true addict fashion, I secretly found the audiobook online, and I was hooked.

Eating disorders are addictive processes, though this was never mentioned to me during my first attempt at recovery three years ago. I had just admitted for the first time that I had a problem, and I found a program that I thought would address it. This would have been great, except the program only addressed my eating habits and body image issues; my history of pills, pot and partying were barely mentioned. After the allotted ten weeks at the center, I had gained a few pounds but still had all the same behaviors—except now I was more aware of them, which meant I felt crazier than ever. I couldn't go back to the denial I clung to during my adolescence, when I refused to even consider that anorexia could be the cause of my low body weight and paralyzing fear of food, but I had no idea how to move forward with this knowledge. I was stuck, hating my life, feeling inept at my job and miserable in my long-term relationship. I heard all that in *Eat Pray Love*; I heard about my own life as I listened to Elizabeth's words. I heard about my love of school, writing, yoga, meditation, men. I even heard about my trip to Russia when I was sixteen!

I started having an intense urge to travel, and somehow I knew that this wasn't just about going on some trip. I needed to get out of my life and out of myself. I needed to change. But that was easier said than done. As unhappy as I was, I was also committed to the life I was living, and I didn't want to give it up.

My boyfriend and I had recently moved to a cute mountain home, adopted a dog and told ourselves our life was perfect, even though the reality was far from it. I was baffled and terrified; I would wake up hysterical, wanting to die; stare at the refrigerator, shaking with fear; and hide in my office, sobbing uncontrollably. I would go to bed vowing that I wouldn't get high tomorrow, and soon after waking, I'd find myself sitting with my pipe in my hand and my heart on the floor. But that's addiction for you.

During this time, I clung to *Eat Pray Love* like a life preserver. I didn't know what else to do, so I just started trying things in the book, like meditating with the Gurugita. I began praying to a God that Elizabeth helped me wrap my head around. Every day, I stared at the Buddhist saying posted on my wall, "When the student is ready, the teacher will appear," and thought, "Okay, God, I'm ready. I don't know what I need, but I know I need it."

Then, I collapsed. Denial of my situation had become harder and harder, and I began to see I wasn't the only one hurt by my self-destruction. My boyfriend was bewildered and heartbroken; he wanted to help but was as powerless as I was over my addiction. We loved each other deeply, but my addiction had left enormous pain in its wake. I had to leave so we could both heal ourselves. I still didn't know how to move forward. I just knew I was *done* with life as it was. I was emotionally, spiritually and physically spent. That's when I sat down in the middle of the road, just like Elizabeth, and said, "I cannot go any farther. I need help."

A week later, my very own copy of *Eat Pray Love* in hand (yes, I finally went out and bought the book), I was on my way to a second try at rehab. It was a veritable sanctuary in the woods on Vancouver Island in Canada, and I spent several months there. Intellectually, I chose that particular program because it treats eating disorders and substance addiction as a singular, multifaceted disease, which somehow I knew I needed. Emotionally and spiritually, I was drawn to the island, the trees and the kind nature of Canadians. Having grown up just below the border of British Columbia, I spent a lot of time on the island as a child. Entering treatment there felt like coming home.

When I first arrived, the center took all of my personal effects besides clothing. After about two months, I had begun to open up, was making progress and had integrated into my recovery some of the spiritual tools I had learned from *Eat Pray Love*. I asked to have my book back, and when it was returned to me, I opened to where I left off on the plane—Elizabeth's description of the *kundalini shakti*.

The timing was miraculous. The very next day I was to participate in a sweat lodge—a cleansing and rebirthing fire ceremony. After years of practicing yoga, I vaguely understood the *kundalini shakti* as an enlightening energy that rises up through the spine, depicted by blue light in the third eye; Elizabeth describes how it burns away everything standing between the self and the divine.

During the ceremony, with Elizabeth's words in my head, I prayed harder than I even believed possible and entered a trance, aware only of a blue light in my mind's eye and a feeling of love that enveloped all my cells. When I stepped out of the lodge four hours later, I felt like a phoenix rising from the ashes: the legacy of anorexia, addiction and anguish that I had been shouldering had burned up and fallen away. I was ready for a new beginning.

For most of my life, I was incapable of feeding myself, had no real notion of a higher power and operated entirely from a place of ego and fear. Elizabeth's story taught me that in order to radically change my life, I had to leave everything familiar behind. I had to face and forgive the darkest parts of me. I had to cross over. Elizabeth Gilbert's courage made me brave enough to leave my home, job, partner and country behind to save my life and go to rehab, where I literally learned how to eat, pray and love.

Today, I'm thriving. I celebrated one year of being clean and sober shortly before my twenty-sixth birthday, surrounded by extraordinary love and friendship. I'm learning to love myself, with the help of other recovering addicts, alcoholics and anorexics, and every day I gain a little more freedom from the chains of anorexia. I know I'm one of the lucky ones. I also know I have a lifetime of work ahead of me to stay on this path, and I'm grateful to the universe every day for the opportunity to do just that.

Thank God—and *Eat Pray Love*—for that.

Write It Down

——

Chelsey Everest

When I was growing up, my mother had a special, go-to piece of advice for me, one that she rarely suggested to my sisters because with them, it never worked. As an answer to almost all of my anxieties, she told me to "write it down."

"Write it down" cured high-pitched lunchroom fights with girls at school and assuaged my father's temper after he'd sent me to my room. It quieted me down when I was bored and performing improv for my mother's forced entertainment in the middle of a grocery store aisle.

I would write whatever served my purpose at the time: a letter, a journal entry, a short story, a prayer. I wrote and illustrated my first book when I was five, a completely plagiarized, crayon version of Eric Carle's *A House for Hermit Crab*.

There wasn't much that I couldn't figure out on paper until I turned nineteen and my doctor told me that I was "mildly depressed." I wasn't certain how one measured the extremity of depression or how many degrees separated mildly depressed from clinically depressed from certifiably insane, but I did know that what I'd been feeling was hardly mild. For about a year, I'd found life to be pretty much insufferable. There had been definite factors: I'd just left for college at Boston University, about two hours south of my hometown in southern Maine, and the homesickness was crippling me. The city campus sprawled across the historic Back Bay, bumping up against the Charles River where the crew teams rowed in the fall and spring, and people were everywhere, clambering off the T or filling the crosswalks of Commonwealth Ave. I barely noticed. I had three roommates sharing my penthouse dorm on the eighteenth floor of Warren Towers, overlooking Fenway's Green Monster and the backed-up traffic on the Mass Pike. Every minute I was surrounded by people, constantly elbow-to-elbow with a hundred strangers, and I'd never felt so alone.

There was also the matter of a cheating high school boyfriend who, shortly after I left, started sleeping with a girl my younger sister knew. She was short and spray-tanned and lied when I messaged her from Boston to ask if they'd been fooling around. After that, every girl looked like a liar. Walking to my eight a.m. lectures, I'd scoff at the girls in high heels, their hair and makeup so perfect that it looked like an entire team had flown in to prep them for class while I donned the same pair of bookstore sweatpants I'd been wearing all week.

I willed my jealousy into loathing, my insecurity into spite. I developed a peculiar brand of hypochondria where a common cold quickly escalated to AIDS; I experienced most of my panic attacks on the elevator up to the eighteenth floor. My anxiety approached in sharply increasing waves, growing to sound-crushing breakers in the matter of a minute. It was a high-pitched wail, a banshee in a bloodstained nightgown with the lungs of a siren.

My depression was different. It was monotone; a sad little crumple of dirty laundry with a face made out of denim pockets. When I tried to explain my depression to my parents, I could never muster the intensity to convey exactly how deep I'd sunk inside of myself. To them, it just didn't make sense. It wasn't like I'd experienced some trauma as a child; there was no repressed memory with an uncle or a babysitter, no younger me witnessing a horrific act of violence that robbed me of my older self's happiness. My life had been sunshine and barbecues, two little sisters who followed me everywhere. There were no issues that couldn't be solved by writing it down. But there was no writing down depression. The sickness infected my words, left me sounding wounded and numb. Depression became my ball and chain. All I could do was limp along.

So when my doctor told me I was depressed, I decided it was time to take action. I asked her to prescribe me medication. I didn't tell my mother at first; I knew she'd get a wrinkle in her forehead and ask me if I knew the side effects, the risk of dependency, the chance that I'd begin ideating suicide or lose my sense of humor or become indifferent to life altogether. It wasn't worth explaining that all of those thoughts had already surfaced on their own. All I wanted were answers; I wanted the misery to be chemical. I wanted medicine to prove that sadness went away.

That summer, after transferring back home to my state school and filling my first prescription of Paxil, I came upon Elizabeth Gilbert's *Eat Pray Love* while on a shopping trip with my mom.

"Medicating the symptom of any illness without exploring its root cause is just a classically hare-brained Western way to think that anyone could truly get better," Gilbert wrote, considering in hindsight her choice to take antidepressants. She'd experienced a nasty divorce, followed by an even more intense affair, and felt herself slipping away from the world in the same slow-motion way that a book falls out of your hands in the moments before you nod off. I knew, because I was feeling that, too. Gilbert sought help in a number of different places and expressed her belief that medication should always be paired with therapy. I loved the idea of therapy, but with a new school only a couple months away, I decided to wait until I could see someone regularly on campus. In the meantime, I read.

Delving into Gilbert's memoir depressurized my mind; it provided me with sweet relief from the trappings of an anxious heart. I'd waitress in the mornings at a diner on the harbor and spend the afternoons dozing on my mother's porch swing, reading *Eat Pray Love* until the Maine mosquitoes reminded me to go inside. Gilbert's search for wellness became my search for wellness, and by immersing myself in her journey, I started to consider the root causes of my depression. I followed her to Italy and allowed myself to feel full and content even as anxiety replaced my appetite; I joined her in India and copied Buddhist mantras onto Post-its that covered the wall above my bed; and I landed with her in Indonesia and finally, for the first time in a year, allowed myself to wonder about love and why it hurts women so deeply. Scraps of napkin and dozens of dog-eared corners fattened my paperback until it was wider than its binding. I would pore over that book with an intent patience until, hours later, I'd look up from the swing and the sky would be tie-dyed purple, my heart beating slowly and my breath coming steadily. This, I know now, was the closest I'd ever come to actually meditating.

After that summer, whenever I found myself in need of guidance, I'd turn time and again to women's memoirs. Slowly I began to see patterns in the way that these writers, and women everywhere, dealt with issues of mental health and sexuality. I would think back on the girls from the lunchroom and the girls from BU in their high heels, and I'd feel a prickling along my arms, a hotness in my chest. In those moments, I felt—was it possible?—compassion. It took a few years (and still, it's rarely easy), but eventually I got to a place where I could begin, again, to write it down. When I turned twenty-five, I enrolled in an MFA program and knew before arriving to my first residency that I would study creative nonfiction and memoir. Now, I facilitate a writing workshop for women. We focus specifically on what has silenced us: what in our lives has left us voiceless, monotone, shrieking or quiet. I urge them to read books by women who have experienced their same pain and come out the other side. I remind them that we all share in suffering. And when one of the writers asks me how I found the courage to write my own difficult stories down, I tell her right away: *Eat Pray Love* made me do it.

Me Time

———

Theressa Real

E*at Pray Love* has been changing lives and rocking worlds for ten years now, but I came to it relatively late, a Liz Gilbert newbie in September 2013.

As the product of a fairly liberal, transient upbringing, I never thought I'd find myself living in the South. But after an apartment fire left me homeless in 2005, I hopped on a bus and followed my mother to a small town in Tennessee. I was young, barely nineteen, and pregnant with my first child. The first person I met after stepping off the bus was the man who would become my husband. He lived across the hall from my mother and me, and you could attribute our friendship and subsequent relationship both to our physical proximity and the general lack of entertainment in town. We passed the time with each other, sharing music, poetry and ideologies.

By 2008, we were married, and my life consisted of working long hours and tending to my husband, our children and various members of his family who lived with us from time to time. For as long as I had known him, my husband had had a dark outlook on life. He was distrustful of any new friendships I made, whether online or through my eighty-hour workweeks. Books became my escape from a painfully isolated reality, but I never quite felt like I deserved to dream of something more than a life spent caring for my family in this little, backward town.

That same year, my husband enlisted with the Army Reserves. He would be gone for six months for basic training, and I remember breathing a sigh of relief at the prospect of being away from him for any length of time. When he returned, he seemed even more controlling than he'd been before. I had recently been laid off, and though I was receiving unemployment benefits, it was nowhere near enough money to support a household. For the first time in our relationship, my husband had complete control of the finances, the house and me.

There had to be more to my life than this, I thought. While my husband was away, I had discovered positive psychology and the power of your own thoughts. I started reading Thich Naht Hahn and Rhonda Byrne, authors who offered a lit path out of my own dark forest. I realized that I *did* deserve to dream of something more. That I wanted a life full of friendships and experiences. In fact, like my husband, I wanted to join the military! I felt it would give me purpose and direction, and would show my daughters that women could do anything they wanted to do.

Of course, my husband couldn't stand the idea of me having any sort of freedom outside the home, and I had to fight tooth and nail to be able to enlist. Eventually, I won that battle, but I was tired of the fighting.

My husband wasn't my only obstacle—my weight was another. I had been overweight all my life, and having recently had a baby meant I was even more out of shape. It took the better part of a year to get fit, but I ultimately enlisted in March 2011 and left for basic training four months later. Meanwhile, the fighting and mistrust between my husband and me continued, made even more pronounced by the distance that is part and parcel of military life. In November of that year, I asked for a divorce.

I thought escaping my husband would help me find myself—that I would become centered and start living the life *I* wanted to live. Unfortunately, it wasn't that simple. I'd been on my own (with custody of my rug rats) for almost two years, and I still didn't feel like I knew who I was, what I was doing or that I belonged anywhere in the world. I was a newly divorced full-time mom of three, trying to figure out my military career while still being a devoted parent, sister, daughter and friend. I wasted so much time comparing myself to everyone around me, trying to prove to myself that I was *good enough* or just *enough*. My chaplain told me I needed to be kinder to myself—something that was easier said than done.

Still, it was with the chaplain's words in mind that I noticed Julia Roberts's face jumping out at me one afternoon in the grocery store, amidst the other five-dollar movies in the overflowing movie bin. I grabbed *Eat Pray Love*, a bag of Twizzlers and a pizza. Mama was going to have herself some me time.

At that point, I knew nothing about *Eat Pray Love* other than that it revolved around three things I love: yoga, food and words. I wasn't prepared for how much Liz's desperation in her marriage, her listlessness with life and her inability to keep herself from jumping into another doomed relationship would speak to me. When she described herself as being a "permeable membrane"—disappearing into the person she loves, giving them everything and keeping nothing for herself—it was like preaching to the choir.

I bought the book not long after watching the movie, and I've since read it more times than I care to admit. On the nights when I've felt so alone and consumed by the dark that the idea there would ever be any happiness again seems like just a willful fantasy, Liz's mantras are what get me through. Just as she reminded herself that she had never really been alone—that that was impossible, because she had herself, and she loved herself—I do the same. I need that reminder—and not from a man, either. Not through being in a relationship. I need to hear it from myself.

My journey still isn't over. Learning to love yourself the right way takes more than just a few therapy sessions, more than a dozen yoga classes. It means more than accepting the first man who comes along willing to share your bed. I remind myself every day that within me there is a Goddess who deserves love, compassion and respect because She gives all of those things so freely.

Divine Timing

——

Crystal Gasser

I first read *Eat Pray Love* when I was seventeen. I was going through a breakup and needed some inspiration to get me through the zombie days. The book helped me realize that for as long as I could remember, I had been using relationships with boys to fill a void. Somewhere down the road I had learned that I was somehow lacking, and the only way I knew to validate my worth was in an endless succession of troublesome boyfriends. But it was suddenly evident to me that those boys just weren't doing the trick.

I began to travel, in the only way I could afford at the time: inward. I started writing more. I started making vision boards. I visualized that travel—real travel—would be a big part of my life. I imagined that my free spirit self would take me around the globe, dipping my toe into the religions and spiritual practices of other cultures, no strings attached. It didn't occur to me that I was still just a teenage girl romanticizing another relationship—this time, a relationship with the divine.

At eighteen, in my senior year of high school, I became a convert to the Church of Jesus Christ of Latter-day Saints. The divine relationship I'd been looking for seemed to have literally come knocking on my door, in the form of two missionaries on bikes. The LDS church found me when I was vulnerable and hurting and needing something more. It didn't matter to me that it was unpopular, and in some ways oppressive and extreme. I was willing to surrender to it for the sake of experiencing love.

I started dating a handsome boy named Daniel who'd been born and raised a Mormon and had just finished serving his mission in Brazil. Within a few short months, we were engaged. Walking in my graduation processional, I hid my ring from my best friend of fifteen years, because on some level I knew I had no idea what I was doing, and I knew she knew it, too. Yet I dove into that faith, just as I'd dived into Daniel's arms. Both of them made me feel safe and comfortable.

The hard part wasn't giving up coffee or abstaining from sex. It wasn't devoting every Sunday to worship or preparing for a wedding I wasn't ready for. It wasn't the tithing or the testimonials. Those things were easy. But I was repressing a powerful force within myself—a force that wanted to move, create, dream and travel. It was as if I'd swallowed a large pill that had lodged in my throat, keeping me from speaking and living out my truth. I knew that marriage in this community almost certainly meant children—lots of children, and soon—and that would mean putting all of my dreams on the back burner. Gradually I realized that I did not want to wake up one day like Liz (and millions of other women), with a man I didn't know with 100 percent certainty I could love till "eternity," in a faith to which I did not entirely seem to belong. I had too many doubts and questions, and my questions were seen as Satan's temptations rather than my own intuition, the voice I'd always depended on. The little voice that had once been my salvation was, in the eyes of the church, a sin.

One summer evening as I was riding in my best friend's car, we drove past our former high school. I spotted the window of the classroom where I'd taken a world religions course, the class that had inspired me to become a seeker of divine truth. Had I found it? I didn't think so. I realized that I longed to be honest with myself again about what it was that I truly wanted. I wanted freedom. I wanted to travel. I wanted God but not religion. I wanted to go to college. I wanted self-love. I wanted courage.

That evening, I called Daniel. My hand was sweating as I gripped the telephone and peered at the notes I'd jotted down to remind me how to say it, pressing so hard that the red pen had made holes in my notepad. "I have something I want to talk to you about," I stuttered. He came to pick me up so that we could speak in person, and before I knew it I had handed him back the ring—and the religion, though I retained a strong love for the community I'd been part of for that brief time. I walked away from that chapter with sadness and relief.

Five years later, I'm at a B & B in Napoli, a fourth-floor walk-up where I've arrived four hours early. The window is open, and I can hear old women yelling from their balconies. Some American song is playing in the street. Here in Italy I've had the most exquisite pizza. I've traveled for real now. I have swum in the Mediterranean and dipped my toes in the Adriatic. I have lounged in Paris parks and explored the concept of death in an old castle in Belgium. This past year I've even had the opportunity to travel to Thailand to practice yoga.

Daniel is married now, with three children, and I am incredibly happy for him and his family. As for me, I am just beginning. I don't know where I would be had I not read *Eat Pray Love*, but I imagine it wouldn't be here, on a balcony in Napoli, looking outward and inward with nothing but love.

Playing the Part

Lisann Valentin

I have to quit my job. *I have to quit my job.*

That thought played on repeat as I walked out of my Wall Street office on a sunny Thursday afternoon, tears streaming down my face.

I headed down the block, dodging a crowd of tourists. I needed to get some air, to stop crying and collect myself. Even with the crush of people around me, it was as if I was totally alone. No one cared what I was doing. So I started to pray out loud, asking God, "Is this the right thing to do?"

The very next moment, an answer came down from the heavens (or the windowsill of a swanky office building) in the form of pigeon poop. And through my tears, I burst out laughing. I had my answer.

Lawyers don't just quit their jobs. We're taught to be responsible. We have commitments we can't walk away from—or so I believed. But after years of living a life that did not fulfill me, it was time to make a decision. I could feel it in my heart. I could also feel it on my shoulder.

Growing up, I believed that success was achieved only by following a straight and narrow road. In Latino culture, being the eldest child means you have a duty to pick up where your parents left off when it comes to providing for your family. And that means becoming a responsible—and successful—adult. It means receiving a good education, establishing a stable career, finding a suitable spouse and eventually having children of your own. It does not mean pursuing an artistic career, especially if your parents happen to be city employees who view their creative endeavors as hobbies, not career paths.

So of course, I fell in love with acting—it just took a very long time for me to realize it.

As a child I thought I was destined to be a lawyer. I was inspired by Mrs. Huxtable on *The Cosby Show*. This bilingual sitcom mom was arguing in court by day and running a house full of kids by night. She was a strong, independent woman just like my mom, and she seemed to have it all. *That* was what I wanted. At the time, I didn't see the actress behind the role, and when I acted out scenes from the show, I thought of it as playing, nothing more.

As I got older, people in my life tried to show me that maybe I wasn't just "playing." I never listened. My mother worked her ass off so that I could get a quality education, and I wasn't going to waste that on *the arts*. Instead, I did just as I planned. I majored in English in college—less because I loved to write, though I did, and more because a nun had come to my high school on career day and told us it was the best route for future attorneys. *Perfect*, I thought. Then, at long last, it was on to law school—

where I struggled every single day not to quit. A Puerto Rican girl from Brooklyn, I felt completely out of place among my peers. Still, I refused to give up. I prayed to God every day to help me on my road to "success," happiness be damned. Somehow it didn't occur to me that my misery would follow me after graduation. I thought it was law school that had made me unhappy, not the entire legal profession.

Out in the real world, once again I was determined to make things work. While working as a litigator at a personal injury defense law firm, I networked with other lawyers who seemed to actually enjoy their jobs; I even looked into other areas of law, but every interview revealed I didn't have the experience or connections necessary to make a transition. I was stuck.

Desperate, I made a list in my journal of what might alleviate the unhappiness I was feeling—everything short of making a career change. I wrote, "I want a great apartment, a brand-new car and a loving relationship." I checked off each item within a matter of months. From the outside, I was doing fantastically well! But—surprise, surprise—I still wasn't happy.

I threw up a corkboard in my bedroom and began a vision board. I cut out motivational words from magazines and images of people who inspired me. I thought this might help me discover what I really wanted, what gave me joy. Practicing law clearly wasn't it, and yet I didn't feel ready to give it all up. I had fought so hard to get where I was, and as a reward, I had a great lifestyle. Not a life, mind you, but a lifestyle. I had money to spend on designer bags, impromptu vacations and nights out on the town. I had the respect that comes with being called Counselor. I had the honor my family bestowed upon me for having "made it." How could I say, "This just doesn't fit me anymore?"

Ashamed of what I perceived as my ungratefulness to God—after all, I had begged Him to get me through law school—I stopped praying. I shrugged off the blanket of His love from my shoulders and wrapped myself in my own shabby guilt. I was completely miserable, and I still couldn't figure out what I wanted.

So I started a blog where I chronicled my search for bliss, the writing of which became cathartic, and I began a small book group, thinking it could be another way to find some insight. Our first pick was *Eat Pray Love.* The moment I read these words of Elizabeth's, I was hooked: "I had actively participated in every moment of the creation of this life—so why did I feel like none of it resembled me? Why did I feel so overwhelmed with duty . . ."

Duty. Oh. My. God. That was *me.* Someone else in the world understood what I was going through! I closed the book and held it close to my heart. Even though I wasn't talking to God at the moment, He knew what I needed and found a way to get Elizabeth's story to me.

Despite being raised Catholic, I've always been more spiritual than religious. Ever since an experience I had as a teenager at a Christian retreat, meditation—and the pulse of pure love and peace that came with it—has appealed to me. Elizabeth's experience in the ashram reminded me of this. Maybe meditative prayer could help me find my purpose. And it turns out, the more I meditated, the more I was able to listen to my inner voice. I began to realize that my actual "duty" should be to live a life that fulfills me, no matter what that looks like.

Throughout my journey of self-discovery, watching movies had become a welcome distraction, a way to quiet my mind for a few hours and not obsess over the fact that I didn't know what I wanted. One day, while lying on the couch watching a riveting teen vampire flick, I got lost in thought. I began repeating the lines of the female protagonist out loud, feeling each word as it escaped my lips. Embarrassed, I snapped out of it and laughed at myself. Then, I suddenly remembered I had done this as a child—in fact, had done this for my entire life. One time my boyfriend had even seen me doing it and broke me out of my little trance by saying, "You want to be an actor, don't you?"

At the time I had denied this ridiculous observation. But now I wouldn't. I said out loud, "I think I *do* want to be an actor!"

Then I sat up and asked myself very seriously, "Do you *really*?"

And my inner voice, now stronger than ever, replied with a calm but resounding, "Yes."

Holy crap.

I bolted from the couch into my bedroom and looked at the vision board on my wall. For the first time I saw how all the words, images and phrases I had chosen over the years—words like *film festival*, *writer* and *balance*; photos of actresses I loved—were all physical expressions of my desire to explore and develop my creative side. All this time, some part of me had clearly known what I wanted; I just hadn't been attuned enough to myself to realize it.

To my surprise, my mother was incredibly supportive of my realization, as was my sister, who insisted "she always knew," and my told-you-so boyfriend. I had been wrong. My parents' life, as much as I respected it and the example they had set, didn't have to be my own. I could be a success in a different way. The road, it turns out, wasn't straight and narrow at all. There were forks— if I was brave enough to take them.

I started slowly, just dipping a toe into the pool of professional acting. With each class I took, and every role I booked, I felt a growing sense of peace. Yet I still couldn't bring myself to completely walk away from my legal career.

There were advantages to still practicing law—it meant I brought greater insight and depth to my acting roles. And my life as an actor was making me a better litigator, since I now had a source of joy that powered me through my long days in court. But I was just going through the motions, literally and figuratively. I knew dividing my time this way wasn't going to be possible forever.

Finally, after about three years, I felt ready to stop testing the water. I wanted to swim.

Once I found the courage to ask God for guidance on that random Thursday afternoon, I was ready for the answer that followed. The same week I handed in my resignation letter, I booked the lead role in an off-Broadway play. Soon after, a short film I wrote, directed and starred in was accepted into a film festival. I was offered roles now without even having to audition! And even more important, I was moving people in the way I had dreamed. Audience members actually took the time to tell me how my film resonated with them, how my performance onstage moved them, how they could see I was glowing with happiness.

One year has passed since I said *adios* to the frenzy of Wall

Street (and that cheeky pigeon). Acting and directing, living a creative life that truly fulfills me—that's become my work. *Eat Pray Love* started me down a new path—this time, one of my own making—where I found the courage to follow my heart and not just my head. Thanks, Elizabeth.

Fall Risk

——

Karstee Davis

My best friend sat across the table from me and over happy hour margaritas announced, "You need to read *Eat Pray Love*. It saved my life."

That's a mighty hefty review of a book. I don't know about you, but when someone tells me a book saved her life, I read it.

It was 2009, and I was barely surviving what had been the most horrendous year of my life. I had recently returned to the United States after having been stationed in England for my husband's job. Together, we had decided it would be best if I were in Colorado near my family when he was asked to serve a year in Afghanistan.

Only a few days after saying our goodbyes to each other in Washington Dulles Airport, I found out that I had endometriosis, a painful uterine disorder that can cause fertility issues. I let my husband know over the phone about my diagnosis and the surgery I would need. Shortly thereafter he told me he wanted a divorce. I never found out if it was because of the reproductive challenges we faced, or if he had met someone overseas, or if it was just an amalgamation of moments and conflicts that led to his decision. All I knew for sure was that he had cut off all communication with me and he wasn't coming back.

So there I was: I had no career, having spent my life prioritizing my husband's passion over discovering my own. I was living in my parents' basement, and now I was staring down a difficult surgery to remove the masses that were growing on my ovaries.

The day of my surgery came, and as I sat in the waiting room in the early morning hours, my mother and sister by my side, I kept expecting him to show up. Every time the waiting room door opened, I would turn, thinking somehow it would be him. Of course, it never was.

Soon, a hospital administrator called me into a back room to complete some paperwork. Is this still your insurance? Is this emergency contact information still correct?

I crossed out his name and wrote my mother's information in the margins. Then I went back to the waiting room, tears streaming down my face. My mother began crying, too, and rubbed my back, neither of us saying anything. My sister didn't cry, because she's the strong one, but the look on her face was so intense, I didn't know if she was so mad at him for not showing up, or if she was so scared that someone you love could break you like that.

I watched as a tiny old woman pushed her wheelchair-bound husband to the check-in desk. He was holding her purse and making jokes about how he always has to hold her purse.

After the surgery, as I was waking up in the recovery room, I saw my mother sitting near the bed, watching TV. I looked around and told her how weird it was that men had nipples. Then, a little less loopy, I began to take in all the tubes and wires hooked up to my body, the little fluorescent yellow bracelet wrapped around my wrist that read FALL RISK. The doctors and the nurses told me I had to walk, so I walked past the nursery, looking through the window at all the newborns. They told me I had to shower, so I stood there as my mother washed my hair and body. Eventually, I returned home to my parents' basement and slept. I took Ambien, lots of Ambien. I took baths. I applied for jobs, binge-watched *The Sopranos* and left a trail of margarita salt behind me everywhere I went.

Nearly a year later, I received news from a mutual friend that my husband, the man who had greeted me every morning by whispering "You're my favorite person," had remarried. Soon after hearing this, I had a seizure. Tests were done, and these were the results: I was carrying too much stuff around with me, and the stress was now manifesting itself physically. I had to learn to let it go.

So there I was, post–happy hour drinks, standing in the bookstore, following my friend's recommendation and buying *Eat Pray Love*. Could this book really save my life?

I wish I could say that after finishing it, I was moved to sell all my belongings and go find myself in the world. But that's not what happened.

This is what I did instead: As Liz writes, I prepared for "riotous and endless waves of transformation" and eventually I started to cultivate the practice of picking out my thoughts. I started by keeping a gratitude journal, where I recorded one thing I was grateful for every day. Now, I look back through these journals and laugh at the days where I could find nothing else to be grateful for except the Denver Broncos.

I found a fulfilling job at the University of Colorado in Boulder, working to help send students abroad. With every student who leaves his or her comfort zone and sets out into the world, I can't help but think I'm helping to develop a generation of more compassionate citizens. And as a benefit of working at the university, I was able to take an early morning travel-writing course on campus during summer break. Summers in Boulder are one of Colorado's best-kept secrets: the Flatirons bask in the glory of the morning sun, and most of Boulder's student population has left town. I fell in love with the students who stayed behind and took that class with me; they would show up just out of bed, hair still tousled, and write the most enchanting descriptions of Cuba that I had ever heard. During one workshop session, in front of an entire group of students, I read aloud the most honest piece I've ever written. I couldn't stop the tremors in my voice as I was reading, but it felt good to be creating.

I took a yoga class at Red Rocks Amphitheatre in Morrison one summer morning, as the light crept over the city below. As I flowed into a *chaturanga*, I felt the most delicious burst of forgiveness and gratitude for myself and the man who was once my husband. In the company of two thousand yogis, I silently thanked him for the love that we had while it was good; the little moments that I carry with me: the scratchy good-morning beard nudges, the daisies at that metro stop in Paris, the feel of bare feet dancing on a stone-tiled kitchen floor, the way he always offered his arm when we walked over slippery cobblestones. The nicknames like Blueberry Muffin and My Lady. Afterward, I got in my car, rolled all the windows down to enjoy the sunshine and mountain air and laughed to myself. I felt alive. Finally.

Upon discovering that yoga could really feel that good, I immediately joined a studio. Through my practice, I've learned that no matter what each day brings, my mat is always a fertile place where I can keep growing the person I'm meant to be, the person I'm already becoming.

I'm also a new member of the Auntie Brigade, a term that Elizabeth coined, and it is a role so sweet and rewarding that it fills me up, despite my ovary woes. It shows me I can embrace a different narrative, choose a different path.

Thanks to *Eat Pray Love*, I realized that a whole other life starts after marriage ends, and that there is tremendous value in learning who you are and what you want outside of societal pressures. There are other stories besides "man meets woman, they fall in love, buy a big house in the 'burbs and create lots of mini-me's."

Then there's this.

Weeks after my surgery, I was standing in line in a department store, waiting to pay for my items. As I stepped up to the counter, I exchanged greetings with the cashier, who began scanning and bagging my purchases as I rummaged through my bag for my credit card. When I found it, I reached across the counter to hand it to her, and as I did, my sleeve moved up just enough to expose my wrist.

As she took my card, the cashier asked, "Do you want me to remove that concert bracelet for you? I have some scissors right here."

I looked at my fluorescent yellow hospital bracelet. I didn't feel ready to be unbranded. But I held my wrist out, she slid the pair of scissors around the bracelet and snap!

That's exactly how *Eat Pray Love* made me feel—like I wasn't a "Fall Risk" anymore. For the first time, I knew I could stand on my own.

Good Enough

Laurie Granieri

For one solid week, it is 10:26 in my apartment.

The red clock in the living room has stopped, and it stays stopped. Every time I look, there it is: 10:26, all day long.

Eventually, I unfold the Lilliputian screwdriver on my Swiss Army knife, which also happens to feature a pair of tweezers that keeps my brows from going full-tilt Frida Kahlo. I perform some lefty-loosey action on two stubborn metal screws, pry open the backside of the clock, insert a new battery and make it 8:12.

Before I read *Eat Pray Love*, a week of 10:26 would have been unfathomable. Because 10:26 would exist as a 24/7 reminder that something was wrong, out of place, out of time. Back then, I'd rectify this brokenness by 10:29 at the latest.

Eat Pray Love spurred my conversion from the stringent dogma of Perfectionism to a scrappy faith in Good Enough.

Now, "conversion" doesn't mean I experienced a full-bodied,

come-to-Jesus moment down by the riverside. I did not see The Light. This new approach has emerged in fits and starts. But it's here.

Bruce Springsteen recorded a song in the late '70s called "Ain't Good Enough for You." That poor schlub: He does everything to please his girl. He gets a job in sales, buys a shirt at Bloomingdale's. No dice—she doesn't like the way he walks or the way he talks.

That was my anthem, for decades. Nothing I did was good enough. I was my very own petulant girlfriend, tossing myself to the curb for not being smart enough, quiet enough, Zen enough. *Eat Pray Love* challenged me to sing a different tune.

A little about Perfect and Imperfect: In 2004, within ten weeks, I divorced, sold my house and lost my big brother. I was caught in a tsunami of pain.

Eventually, I began suffering debilitating back pain and twice-weekly migraines. I was working in the crumbling newspaper business, watching helplessly as colleagues were escorted from the newsroom on a regular basis. It was as if I were squirming on an eternal chopping block. Who was next? Joy, even when it did show up, was totally suspect and all too brief.

And because I couldn't control big-ticket items, like death and divorce, my Miss Fix-It urge went to town on little things. (See: compulsive clock-fixing and eyebrow-tweezing.) I was forever anticipating the other shoe, the slippery banana peel. I had elected myself a one-woman vigilante, behaving as if the weight of my anxious attention could remove the sting of life's vicissitudes.

It's easy to forget, but Gilbert embarked on a year abroad with only a dim hope that she'd emerge whole. She didn't know the end of the story. Who could predict a pearl of blue light and a loving Brazilian man, let alone Oprah Winfrey and Julia Roberts?

My own conversion from Perfect to Good Enough involved setting out on a path that held zero guarantees. I always relate to that distressed father in the Bible who cried: I believe; help my unbelief! In other words: I want to trust you, man, but I'm not sure I can put one foot in front of the other. I'm not certain if it's even worth lacing up my boots.

I spend most of my life curled up in that semicolon between "I believe" and "Help my unbelief!" and when I'm there, Gilbert's own uncertainty keeps me company. She had no reason to believe anything would come of this journey, beyond a manuscript and a few passport stamps.

Still, she laced up her boots.

Eat Pray Love nudged me to lace up my own, but at the same time it gave me permission to come undone; to every so often ignore an e-mail, skip a workout, take a nap.

I figured I had good reason to live a righty-tighty life, in which I was forever furrowing my brow, checking my watch and doing my damnedest to reach Perfect by lunchtime. When I was growing up, women who rested seemed depressed. They lay on their right sides atop efficiently made beds and zoned out on *The Price Is Right* and *The Young and the Restless* before returning to the daily business of serving others. Rest seemed akin to giving up.

But Gilbert writes convincingly about rest, and about mothering one's joy—nurturing and protecting it. Sure, Gilbert visited a medicine man, but she administered her own remedy. As for me, my yearlong migraine odyssey involved a neurologist, a Reiki master, two acupuncturists, a handful of chiropractors, staring at mandalas in the local library, screaming in the car (to relieve the pressure—I figured, why not?), a brief hospital stay and a boatload of meds and research before I found a nutrition-ist who was able to alleviate most of my headaches.

Gilbert reminds me that joy doesn't just show up on the front lawn and begin doling out blank checks. Joy must be beckoned. Joy must be tended.

I realize *joy* is a squirrelly word, right up there beside its abused siblings, *mindful* and *empowered*. I don't care. I am committed to the ongoing work of joy, and I don't mean a deaf-and-dumb, smiley-face-emoji brand of joy. I'm talking eyes-wide-open joy that sees the world for what it is and chooses to remain soft any-way. I'm talking about joy despite.

Eat Pray Love did not make me bigger, better, more. Some days reality is all too real. Some days I can be impatient. I fret intermittently over my square toes. The difference is, nowadays I can live with myself.

There's still so much I long to fix. Some are worthy goals (gun laws, those overplucked eyebrows), and others can wait. I have arrived at a shaky but plucky faith in Good Enough. And I plan to keep on arriving, showing up for myself as often as I need to, hour after hour, minute after minute, no matter how long it takes.

Cry Teach Grow

—

Leslie Patrick Moore

When I first read *Eat Pray Love* I devoured the entire book in one sitting. No matter that I was fairly happily married at the time—this woman's tremendous, jet-across-the-world bravery won me over and I fantasized about going on a soul-seeking mission just like hers—without the getting divorced bit. Perhaps I wished a little too ardently, though, because a few years later, the scenario actually came true for me. Though instead of leaving my husband, *I* was the one being left.

I had seen it coming. For seven months we had been dealing with my sudden and painful discovery of his infidelities. We screamed and cursed at each other. *Promise me you won't do it again*, I would shout, begging for an assurance he refused to give. I cried in therapy and drank way too much in order to cope. But deep down, I could feel a massive shift occurring. Like animals can sense a forthcoming earthquake, I could feel divorce lurking. Growing up in a family where one simply doesn't get divorced,

I scarcely acknowledged the possibility, but the inevitability of it shook me off my feet the instant my husband spoke those damning words—*I don't want to be married anymore.*

I have a certain jealous longing when I hear the stories of some divorced couples—that the cheating spouse begged the innocent partner to stay in the relationship; that said cheater promised to stop the heinous extramarital behavior, swore he or she would do anything to save the marriage. To me, that sounded romantic! It meant the spouse still cared, maybe even felt truly remorseful. That he or she would truly make an effort to be present, to change. That there was still love—and the hope of reconciliation.

There was no such hope for us. My husband's uttered words meant it was over, that I was no longer loved, though I still loved him. They meant there was nothing I could do to save our marriage.

I had married young, at twenty-one, going straight from my father's household to my new husband's. He had been my first everything. We were newlyweds when I finished college and began a fledgling career in marketing, writing copy for a local bank, unsure of what I really wanted for my life. My husband became my sole system of support, both emotionally and financially. I was working a full-time job and dabbling in freelance writing on the side, so I had my own money coming in, but most of that I gave to my husband for our monthly bills, and I had no idea what happened to anything extra. He also made significantly more money than I did, so my contribution never seemed to amount to much anyway.

I didn't know how to be in the world on my own. I didn't know how to cook, I couldn't program the DVR, I didn't even

know to whom we paid those monthly bills. I was utterly dependent on him in every way.

So after our marriage fractured, I was adrift. I quit my job
and moved to the East Coast to be closer to my sister. Everything
terrified me. Things that people do on a daily basis, like calling
the cable company or renting an apartment, were seemingly in-
surmountable tasks. Other things petrified me as well. One day,
I was so frightened by the fact that I'd never had sex with anyone
besides my husband that I couldn't get out of bed and decided
that maybe I would remain celibate for the rest of my life.

I had been a respectable married woman all during my twenties. Now at twenty-nine, I was divorced and unmoored in the
world. I didn't know who I was anymore. I felt an urgent need to
leave the country. Sure, my support system was here, but so were
all my memories of my eight-year failed marriage. The thought of
staying sickened me.

For six months, I popped Xanax and Prozac like handfuls of
M&M's, drank bottles of wine a day and cried over every reminder of my past life, waiting for the divorce to be finalized.
When I finally received that paper in the mail, undoing what I
had so happily done with my husband all those years before,
something in me changed. I stopped crying long enough to
think, *I should do the* Eat Pray Love *thing.*

As a now freshly divorced writer, I genuinely related to Gilbert's every word. I, too, cried on my bathroom floor! I, too,
wanted to escape to a foreign land to learn Italian from sexy men
with names like Luca Spaghetti. However, with a writing career
not nearly as developed as Liz's, and a bank account depleted
from making do on a single income plus the plethora of expenses
you incur when splitting with your spouse, jetting over to Italy to

revel in eating seemed completely out of the question—let alone praying and loving.

Then, I remembered a girl I had sat next to on a bus in Cambodia while traveling. She was on vacation from her job teaching English in South Korea. On our daylong ride from Siem Reap to Bangkok she explained to me the perks the job offered and all the money she had been able to save, which she used to fund her frequent trips around Southeast Asia. Listening to her, I had wished I could do something like that but dismissed it as a possibility. After all, my job, mortgage and husband were all waiting for me back home in California.

Still, the idea had stayed with me over time, and now I clung to it vehemently, certain it was my ticket to a new, adventurous life. No matter that my teaching experience was nonexistent and I was shy speaking in front of groups. It wouldn't be quite the same as a stint in Italy, India and Indonesia, but it was a perfect way to get a free ticket overseas. All the recruiting company asked was that I be a native English speaker with a college degree. Two weeks after my divorce was finalized, I found myself in South Korea.

I was mesmerized by the experience of living alone. I was mesmerized by the overwhelming sense of foreignness I experienced each time I stepped out of my small apartment. I was mesmerized by my new teaching job. In fact, everything mesmerized me. To say that I "found" myself through this experience may be trite, but it's also true.

In Korean culture, people are defined by things like age, job title and marital status. My middle-school students would constantly ask me if I was married. No, I would respond. You have boyfriend? they would continue. No, I am single. I repeated this phrase, *I am single*, countless times during the first few months, and each time I spoke the words, their palpability became more absolute. I am single. I am not defined by my husband.

Living in a country so obsessed by marriage reinforced my singleness, but I was now existing and even thriving on my own and I loved every minute of it. I learned that I could live by myself, pay my own bills and even be intimate with someone besides my husband—I wasn't going to spend the rest of my life celibate after all! I was shocked to find that the things I dreaded most were the very things that turned out to be the easiest to overcome. After a few months, I, like Liz, even met my own tall, dark and handsome stranger—though mine is English and didn't happen to run me down with his car.

I had done what I set out to do. What I thought was the end of my world morphed into a whole new beginning. I may have eaten kimchi and rice instead of pizza and gelato along the way, but I still had my very own *Eat Pray Love* happy ending. Thanks for the inspiration, Liz.

Crossing Over

Sondra Imperati

T he first time I started *Eat Pray Love* I ended up putting it back on the bookshelf. Liz was in India at the ashram. She had just met Richard and been nicknamed Groceries.

Yes, I put it down.

Richard forced Liz to take a really hard look at herself. If I kept reading, I realized I might have to do the same. At that time, I couldn't handle what *Eat Pray Love* represented, those messages of honoring your truth and embracing fear. I was stuck in my life, moments away from my own bathroom breakdown. I just couldn't admit it.

To the outside world, my life looked pretty good. I had a handsome husband, a beautiful home and fancy cars. My career was smoking hot. My husband and I acted happy, so of course others thought we were.

Then there's what goes on behind closed doors.

For many reasons, I couldn't trust my husband. And he resented that I was a workaholic who didn't care for myself. The Italy part of *Eat Pray Love* had resonated with me and not just because I was Italian. I also had the "eat" aspect down pat. In fact, I was morbidly obese. Still, as crazy as it sounds, most of the time we were friends and enjoyed each other's company. We tried to love and support each other the best we could. In the end, though, we became casually indifferent.

Even more than before, food and work were now my coping mechanisms. I relied on them to distract me from the pain, shame and loneliness I was feeling, when in reality I was slowly killing myself, one solitary binge at a time. This became crystal clear when, in an overdue visit to my doctor, the wake-up call of high blood pressure sounded.

I had to take back my health.

I began keeping a journal and started to understand my triggers for emotional eating. I read books and learned to eat clean. I exercised at home for fifteen minutes each day. Then thirty minutes, then an hour. I worked with a trainer in my house, then graduated to a gym with classes and trainers. And very slowly I started to like this woman who woke up at five a.m. to care for herself.

It was around this time Liz came back into my life, in the form of Julia Roberts.

My husband bought me the DVD of *Eat Pray Love* as a present, and we watched it together. At the end of the movie, I excitedly asked him what he thought of it.

He replied that he hated it; that Liz was selfish to leave her husband.

I didn't say a word. I went upstairs, dusted off my copy of the book, and this time I stayed up all night reading it cover to cover. I couldn't put it down. I was so moved by Liz's courage to live her truth and tell her story.

As I lost more weight, I started to unearth other hidden layers of myself. I pursued dreams I never thought I could achieve. I took a flight lesson, dabbled in tennis and heated yoga. I gained some self-respect. And somewhere along this journey of my eighty-pound weight loss and mission of self-discovery, I encountered "the soul mate" who would break me open.

It was a deliberate, calculated seduction on his part, and while nothing ever happened physically, I'm sorry to admit I was an eager participant. I was in a dying marriage, and my "soul mate" taught me it was okay to show vulnerability and ask for help. He stimulated a thirst for knowledge and learning that I had never experienced before. The highs were higher than I had ever known. The lows brought a despair I could never have fathomed. Liz was right. It couldn't and didn't last.

During this time, I came to realize my marriage was truly over. After twenty years together, I initiated the divorce, sold the house and left my job all at the same time. It's no wonder that when I finally hit the bathroom floor I hit it hard.

I lost twenty more pounds because I stopped eating and instead cried constantly. I took to my bed in my new apartment and stared at the ceiling most days, desperately praying to God for help and protection. I felt more alone and exposed than I ever had in my life.

When I finally managed to venture out into the world again, I was an unrecognizable, emotional wreck. My faithful friend Colleen said it best: "Sondra, your eyes are dead."

At breakfast one morning she told me, "You've left your marriage, your home, your job—most people drink, drug or sex their way through any one of these events. You're experiencing all of them at the same time and are doing none of that. You need to go to the doctor. I'll go with you. Take something to help yourself."

The next day I made an appointment with my gynecologist. He had been with me through three miscarriages, and I thought he would be more understanding than my general practitioner.

I told him everything and asked for something to take the edge off.

He hesitantly offered, "I could put you on Paxil."

"Paxil?" I muttered.

He moved closer and said, "Sondra, I'm really sorry for all you are going through. You're going to be okay. Get your ass back to the gym for forty minutes a day. Start eating. Trust me."

I took his advice. I went home and changed. After sitting in the parking lot for about an hour, I went into the gym. I gingerly stepped on the elliptical. After forty minutes I had to admit I felt a little better.

I kept going back to the gym.

I began to eat again.

My prayers became more hopeful.

Slowly, I was learning to love and accept myself. I had no choice.

Since I was a little girl, I've listened to music and I loved to sing, be it in musicals, choirs or along with the radio in the car. I appreciate the melodies, but as an avid reader fascinated by all types of language, what I really connect with are the lyrics.

I decided I needed to reignite my passion in a new way. I

loved listening to the gospel choir during Mass and feeling the music inside myself. I longed to join the choir but was too afraid to go on my own.

One day, not long after I came to that realization, my path crossed with Mary Lou, a former colleague and my dear friend. As we were catching up, I learned she was a gospel singer at my church. I told Mary Lou I wanted to sing in the choir but that fear was stopping me. She just looked at me and said, "You're coming with me." Without hesitation, I followed her.

That very night, I met Michael for the first time. My Brazilian turned out to be a divorced Irish/German American with three children and a grandson on the way!

I grew up an only child and dreamed of having a family. When all my pregnancies ended in miscarriages, I was both devastated and oddly relieved. Oddly relieved, because it turns out I was terrified at the prospect of having children. I realize now that those fears were directly tied to my doubts about my marriage. If those babies had been born, I never would have left.

My dream of a family did end up coming true—just not in the way I had imagined as a child. I love Michael's family like they are my own: his son Matthew and daughter-in-law Haylee, his beautiful grandson, MJ, and his daughter, Stephanie, who sang in the church choir and had been helping to play matchmaker behind the scenes, unbeknownst to me.

Michael loves wine and is a gourmet cook. He also enjoys music, and we take the time to appreciate it together as often as we can.

Our shared faith and love for God and our church is an important bond that strengthens us as individuals and partners. Sometimes I watch Michael pray, and in those quiet moments I could not feel closer to him and to God.

And then there's love. I have never experienced this type of genuine, unconditional acceptance from a man. I'm learning that truth, honesty and communication—even when it's hard—are cornerstones to enduring love, intimacy, passion and connection.

I believe things happen for a reason. Michael encourages me to keep writing even when I'm afraid—something Liz also does, on Facebook and in her Magic Lessons podcast series. I listened—and I got to work.

Running on My Own

—

Elizabeth Duffy

I was twenty-three years old and two years sober the first time I read the book that would change my life.

I had been abusing substances since the age of twelve. Being intoxicated for the better part of your formative years is not a great way to learn about who you really are and what you want out of life. But I was making progress. I finished college and was starting to earn back my family's trust. And I was detoxing off my final vice—a five-year-long destructive relationship with my codependent savior.

The codependent and the addict—what a horror story. I felt a certain loyalty to him because he had stayed with me during my darkest hours. How could I repay that by getting sober and just walking away?

My friends lovingly reminded me that I needed time and distance away from him; I needed to figure out who I was on my own. If I did the work and still felt we should be together, then fine, get back together. But not before.

The "work" turned out to be a long road, and breaking away from that relationship was just the start of my journey. I never picked up a substance again, but I kept picking up men who I thought could save me. My sense of my self-worth was completely lacking, and so I tumbled through one terrible relationship after another. That, it turns out, was the crux of all my issues, the reason I drank and numbed. I didn't know how to stand on my own.

I bought *Eat Pray Love* at Target. I remember seeing the cover and thinking how beautiful it was—love at first sight. And with each page I read, I felt Elizabeth Gilbert was uncovering parts of myself that I had been scared to see. She refused to deny her truth, and that inspired me and filled me with hope. I realized that it was time for me to finally cross the street and walk in the sunshine. I owed it to myself and no one else.

I began to make plans to move to Thailand and became certified to teach English as a second language. It was June, and by September I would be financially stable enough to go. But as someone once said, "We make plans and God laughs." In July, I was contacted by a potential employer with the offer of my dream job—to work for the same drug and alcohol rehabilitation center I had been treated at. Conflicted, I called my father. He had been very supportive of my move to Thailand and was excited for me to take this step. As I spoke to him about the offer, though, he became quiet. Then he responded with words I didn't expect. "Elizabeth, I know you wanted to go to Thailand to work. But if you take this job, in some time you will be able to go to Thailand on vacation." I took the job and put Thailand on hold.

I will never be able to truly convey how much that job did for me. Being around addicts in their first days of sobriety gave me a whole new appreciation for my own recovery. I realized how incredibly lucky I was. My once shameful past was now a story of inspiration for young people who were able to say, "If she can do it, maybe I can." I felt fulfilled, proud of the work I did and the impact I was able to have. Yet my wanderlust was always tugging at my soul; I still dreamed of Thailand.

I was also repeating my most destructive pattern.

I said yes to a marriage proposal. I was twenty-seven now, surrounded by friends who were getting married. Even though I felt myself fading, I stayed in the relationship and lived his dream for a few months, believing that I owed him this in exchange for the ring he gave me and the life he promised. I would wake up in cold sweats in the middle of the night. Something was horribly wrong. I had the perfect guy but was desperately unhappy.

No longer being able to deny my truth, I reread *Eat Pray Love* and found myself again through Elizabeth's words. "Never again use another person's body or emotions as a scratching post for your own unfulfilled yearnings." I gave back the ring.

It is still astonishing to me how, at the exact second we stop trying to make something fit, room opens up for what was meant to be there all along. For me, this came in the form of an ultramarathon in Egypt. By participating in this race, I would be able to travel while also raising money for the treatment center where I worked. I completely committed myself. The training schedule was grueling, not allowing me time for anything besides work and running. And it was through this training that I finally broke my habit of jumping from relationship to relationship. I was running, but for the first time I wasn't running away from anything. I was running to find myself.

During the race, I met many wonderful people from all over the world. We bonded in exhaustion and pain. A British man in particular was there filming a documentary on a group of Aussies who were running the race to raise awareness for diabetes. I had no intention of trying to meet a man in the Sahara—especially since we were all peeing in the sand, unshowered, and wearing the same clothes 24/7. Yet William kept coming over and initiating conversations.

At the end of the week, back at our hotel in Cairo, we all changed into clean clothes and ate a final meal together. I was on such a high, surrounded by new friends, proud of my achievement and feeling a newfound gratitude for soap. I had also never been so tired in my life, but I stayed up all night in the lobby with William. We talked about the lives we were returning to—mine in Florida and his in New Zealand. We exchanged information so we could keep in touch. There was something special about him, but I didn't kid myself that he would become anything more than a great pen pal. At four a.m., he helped me carry my bags to the taxi and we hugged. As I got into the car, I was caught off guard by a wave of sadness when I realized I would probably never see him again. Then I did my best to shake it off and fell asleep. I returned to Florida, and life carried on.

Much to my surprise, William wrote me. We exchanged daily e-mails, and he became one of my dearest friends. We would tell each other about our days on the opposite sides of the world, always keeping it light and casual, with zero expectations.

One day I opened an e-mail from him. Do you want to be my date to my friend's wedding next month? Sure! I responded without hesitation and asked where it was. Thailand, he said. Thailand! I said yes and finally made it to the destination of my dreams. Almost three years later, William is my best friend and the love of my life. I know I would never have met him if I hadn't done the work and learned how to stand (and run) on my own.

As Elizabeth wrote, I made space for the unknown future to fill up my life with yet-to-come surprises. I'm so grateful that *Eat Pray Love* made me do it.

"Read Me Your Story, Mandy"

Amanda Whitten

W hen I was eight years old and obsessed with *The Baby-Sitters Club, Nancy Drew*—anything, really, that smelled of paper and was composed of chapters—I wrote my own stories. A series called Friends Forever, the beginnings of a murder mystery novel, melodramatic poems, songs I had no business "singing." I wrote. I told people I wanted to be an author when I grew up.

Every Saturday I wrote in the backseat of my family's '84 Chevy Blazer while we made the predawn fifty-mile trek from Bakersfield to an even sleepier central California town to help my grandpa, where he rented a busy corner spot at the Porterville swap meet. After a sweaty morning selling wicker furniture, stuffed animals, candy bars and books, hustling for every penny, Grandpa would pull out his lunch, sit in his truck and ask me to read him my latest story.

Somewhere between childhood and womanhood I stopped

writing my own words and just started adopting the stories oth-ers told. I could say I got too busy. That "life" got too busy. First there was college, part-time jobs, the collapse of my parents' marriage and the pieces my dad left for us to pick up like an in-complete jigsaw puzzle you'd find at a neighborhood yard sale. Then my own mismatched marriage, the all-consuming nature of law school, career and a series of thoughtless choices that landed me in increasingly regrettable situations. But the truth was, I had just lost the courage to write. There is something about growing up that can destroy us. Something about building a life that can tear down a soul.

For a time I had even stopped reading. Reality television and *Us Weekly* were the most culture any of my days held.

But then I left my marriage, my house and my five-year plan. Life doesn't always give us second chances, so I took the chance to find myself again, and I'm not even embarrassed by the cliché of it. I guess you could say *Eat Pray Love* made me do it.

I drove myself across Ireland on the wrong side of the road and brought home a long-distance love affair, the only souvenir that's ever broken my heart. I climbed an active volcano in Quito, Ecuador. I found the gelato shop in Florence where Elizabeth Gilbert discovered the frozen rice pudding that made her proclaim she wouldn't go to heaven if it wasn't there. I dragged my mom on a road trip to bear witness to nine innings of baseball in seven of the major league stadiums from Boston to Chicago. I bought a condo, sight unseen, and remodeled it with my own two hands (and a good deal of stupid questions to Home Depot employees). I crossed the finish line of an Iron-man triathlon after fourteen hours and twenty-three minutes of consecutive exercise. I adopted two cats and embraced the stigma that comes with being an unmarried lady of marrying age with cats.

But first, I put down the television remote and picked up a book. Any book. Fifty-two of them a year to be exact, because I'm big on goals. I remembered that I loved escaping into words. I found writers whose words comforted me. Elizabeth Gilbert. Cheryl Strayed. Ann Patchett. Other women who had left marriages when they were too young to explain it away with a midlife crisis. Other women who had to admit "defeat" and then reclaim it as their awakening. I adopted their words. Their stories were so similar to mine.

I s that one of the stories you wrote, Mandy?" Once again, it was my grandpa asking. But I wasn't a child, and we weren't in California anymore. We were somewhere between Albuquerque, New Mexico, and the worst Mexican restaurant ever to land in a travel guide. We were taking Grandpa, now two weeks shy of eighty and battling Alzheimer's, on a road trip to Enid, Oklahoma, to see his baby sister for the first time in at least fifteen years and, though we didn't know it at the time, the last. And it wasn't one of my stories I was reading, though I was certainly enjoying it. The words resonated with me. But they still weren't mine.

These are.

Just a few months later, my grandfather died. We buried him under an old oak tree on a warm July day. But out on that desert highway, despite the confusions of Alzheimer's, my grandpa had remembered that I was a writer. And suddenly, so had I.

Answering the Call
of the Higher Self

—

Billy Rosa

I t's broken." Those words from the X-ray technician changed
everything. What I heard him say was, *Your career is over.
You will never dance again. You're worthless.* An hour before
this, two friends had carried me out of a Broadway audition after
a loud snap of my hip rendered me unable to stand, let alone
walk. The choreographer had asked if I could jump into a split
midair and then land into one on the ground. Sure! I had just
done this for three months, seventeen times per week, as a cho-
rus dancer for the Radio City Christmas Spectacular. Little did I
know, my final bow as a dancer would be crawling on a New
York City sidewalk from a yellow cab to the entrance of the
emergency room.

I had been a professional dancer for years; I owned and
breathed it. It informed every moment of my life, and the truth
was, I knew nothing else. By the young age of twenty-three, I

had used dancing to define every aspect of who I was. I was my high kicks and multiple turns; I was my splits and backbends; I was what I could do for you onstage. I was fully identified with my body, craft and ego. Lying in that hospital bed with a fractured hip, I no longer knew who I was. I couldn't even stand my own company.

It was during this period of loneliness and self-loathing that a friend suggested I read *Eat Pray Love*. Liz's story changed the way I saw and experienced myself. In a moment when my heart felt as cracked as my body, Liz ushered in a new possibility. There was love and excitement, of course, but dancing had also allowed me to avoid life and remain transfixed on the image in the mirror. As long as the music kept playing, I never had to take responsibility for being a whole, fully functioning human being in the world. I had become a machine. Now, I had a choice to make. I could stay on this path and settle for the self-created limitations I'd always known, or I could start over and reengage life as someone new.

Eat Pray Love encouraged and guided me to my decision. Liz's determination to open and heal her heart taught me that not only am I the hero of my own life, but I better get about living it. So, I learned to meditate and practiced being with myself. I sat in silence and wrote and repeated affirmations. I realized I was so much more than my body. I stopped obsessing over what I was supposed to be and started trying on a different way of being.

I became a student of change, of boldness, of healing. If I could heal my own body, I wondered, how could I help others to heal theirs? I went to massage therapy school and rediscovered the wonder of the human body. Then I enrolled in nursing school, inspired by the client outcomes I witnessed as a massage therapist. I spent four years as a critical care nurse at the bedside, caring for patients who have honored my life with the humble privilege of knowing them. I held the hand of many as they transitioned at end of life and witnessed the tremendous courage and fierce determination of the human spirit. My work as a nurse has been a service to others but also a soulful healing for me. As Ram Dass says, "We're all just walking each other home." Human caring and compassionate loving-kindness are the most life-giving offerings we can make at the feet of another.

I've spent the last few years doing all of the things that "Billy doesn't do." I've received my master's degree in nursing and am planning to pursue doctoral studies in public health. I've trekked to the source of the holy Ganges River at Gomukh Glacier in the Himalayas. I've studied with Shipibo shaman healers in the jungles of the Amazon. I've sat and drunk tea in the home of a gracious mother in an undertraveled province of northern Vietnam. These days, I work and teach in Rwanda, supporting nurses to realize their own healing potential and purpose.

It wasn't *Eat Pray Love* that made me do all this; it was Liz. Liz's words have returned me to myself, showing me how to transform a fracturing experience into a life of wholeness and authentic expression. Her vulnerability has helped recalibrate my cells so I can be a conduit for my inner hero. Her courage has elevated my very being, and her sense of adventure has awakened me to more fully embrace the possibilities of my becoming. I've learned that, no matter how bruised and shaken we may feel, we are never truly broken. We are simply being presented with the experiences we need to realize our greatest Self.

I once met Liz at a book signing and said, "Liz, my name is Billy Rosa, and I don't think I could ever explain to you how your words have changed my life." She held my hands, shared my tears for a brief moment and said, "You just did."

Second-Act Singer

———

Theresa Thornton

In September 2008, when I was forty-seven years old, I sang in front of an audience for the first time in my life.

That summer, my son was learning to play the guitar. He was a sweet, shy boy with a real affinity for music. He was also about to start high school, and I was afraid his timidity would keep his talent hidden. I told my son he had a gift; he was too skilled to be playing music alone in his room. He had to find his tribe in high school—he needed to share himself with the world.

After that talk, I thought about my own life. Who was I? What was my passion? I was a divorced, single mom. The most courageous thing I'd ever done was admit I wasn't happy in my marriage (I left it in the late '90s). But I didn't do much to feed my soul. Post-divorce, consumed with financial and time-management struggles, my life consisted of my two children and my office job. Still, I knew there was more out there—I heard the whisper.

My lifelong fantasy was to be a singer. In grammar school, everyone had a favorite Beatle. I wanted to *be* a Beatle. Sure, I sang in the car alone, but the thought of singing in front of someone, anyone, was terrifying. My dream was so private and closely guarded that no one had ever heard me.

I'd read *Eat Pray Love* two years before encouraging my son to follow his musical passion, and I was inspired. I'd absorbed every drop of Elizabeth Gilbert's life-changing personal journey like she was a friend, talking to me in confidence. As I watched my son follow his artistic ambitions, I knew it was time for me to pursue my own.

I had heard of a daylong workshop at a place in New York City called New York Open Center. The workshop was taught by a successful vocal coach and geared toward finding your voice. I scraped the money together and went on a Saturday morning. I didn't tell a single soul. I figured, if it went badly, no one had to know.

There were about twenty-five people in this workshop, and we all came prepared to sing one song of our choice. As we settled in, we were all given index cards and told to write down why we were there and what we were hoping to gain from the class. I wrote down my goal: I was there to get over my fear of singing in public. Then we did exercises designed to reduce self-consciousness. For example, in pairs, we stared into each other's eyes while making faces and singing. Some found it very difficult and started crying. Staring at another person, at length, makes it impossible to hide your emotions; you feel very exposed and vulnerable.

After lunch, it was time. We all, one by one, had to get up in front of the entire group and sing. The vocal coach pulled from our index cards randomly to determine who would go next, and read each person's goal aloud. Some were singers who had given it up, some were working vocalists who had lost their spark—we all had different reasons for being there. When my name was called, I felt surprisingly calm as I walked to the front of the room. The instructor read: "Theresa wants to get over the fear of singing in public." He asked if I had sheet music or a CD to sing to, and I said no.

With that, I sang—a cappella—the Gladys Knight and the Pips hit "I've Got to Use My Imagination." My voice didn't crack or quiver. It rang out in the room. For a second, I couldn't believe it was me. I was out of my body, watching myself. When the song was over, I looked around the room to astonished faces and open mouths. The vocal coach smiled. He didn't tell me to take vocal lessons—he told me to find a band and get out there.

I was high. I had never felt such singular elation. After the workshop, people came up to congratulate me. One quiet, awkward man who'd sung an almost painful version of "Love Me Tender" told me I was the best thing about his day. He told me I was wonderful, and I felt wonderful.

I had officially begun my journey.

That workshop was just the first step. I took some vocal lessons to get comfortable with singing. Then I met some musicians. I joined my first band. Then another band. And another. My voice has gotten better, stronger. I take more risks. Some work out, some don't. I've had delightfully transcendent moments singing, along with tough patches where I've questioned myself. I've hit some obstacles and criticism that temporarily slowed me down but did not discourage me. I'm fifty-four years old, and I know I'm not going to be the next Etta James. But it's not about that. Singing fills my soul and makes me happy. I sing for me.

My Superstorms

Cara Bradshaw

When Superstorm Sandy hit New Jersey, I was in the midst of a major life transition. I had decided to make a career change and leave my job as a local newspaper reporter for a fund-raising position at my alma mater. And, as Sandy bore down on us, I also decided to jump ship from my marriage. My husband didn't hit me. He didn't cheat. But I felt like I was suffocating. Between covering stories about a couple killed by a fallen tree and locals hunting for nonperishables in dark grocery store aisles, I camped out on the floor of a hotel lobby, lived out of my car and told myself I was making the right choice.

A year into our marriage my husband had admitted he didn't like my latest choice of pleasure reading: *Eat Pray Love.* "You'll read this and think you need to 'go find yourself.'" I laughed. I was twenty-three and had just quit my job at UNICEF so he could take a yearlong rotation in Arizona. I had agreed to the move—it seemed like a good opportunity. But I had also spent my first year as a newlywed frequently alone because of his travel schedule and was hopeful that this next year in a new place would be different. It wasn't. He worked long hours. I got sick and suffered from debilitating anxiety. I craved intimacy and emotional trust. My now ex-husband is a lovely person, but we never cemented the relationship in those first crucial years. We didn't have a fighting chance.

Getting married just months after college graduation didn't seem like the craziest thing I could do. My parents divorced when I was a teen, and I moved with my mother and sisters to low-income housing in a neighborhood once known for addiction and violence. I bounced between my parents' places. My father, a well-respected pastor, took a desk job in IT. My mother, a strong woman who hadn't completed college and stayed home with us, drove a school bus and worked as a teaching assistant. We worried about money. I longed for stability and a sense of "home" again. My fearless self wanted to join the Peace Corps; the scared girl in me needed shelter and security. I chose the latter.

By the time I was in my mid-twenties, I had most of the things I thought I wanted and needed. But at my core I was unsettled and lonesome. When my husband and I moved back to New Jersey from Arizona, I enrolled in graduate school. By the second year of my program, we had become platonic housemates. I needed to believe there could be more. I moved out and rented a room to work on my thesis about post-conflict Nepal. I started seeing someone else. I told my husband I couldn't stay in the marriage. He grew despondent. The few people who knew what was going on told me I was making a huge mistake if I chose to leave my husband and that they wouldn't support me if I did. Plagued with guilt and feeling a responsibility to "stick it out," I moved back in and kept my desires hidden. Not wanting our marriage to be seen as a failure, my husband and I acted as if everything was fine. We lived in limbo for years. We bought a house. It didn't fix a thing. Three marriage counselors couldn't unwind the mess. And no one—despite their ability or inability to love you the way you need to be loved—deserves that kind of torture. I realize now that the feeling of choking that spurred me out of the house years later on that stormy October night was the noose I'd tied around my own neck.

Just when I thought I should do my "Liz Gilbert," as I called it, and pack it up for the other side of the world (Nepal, maybe), my grandmother's health began to decline. A Montanan who studied Russian literature at Stanford and took a train alone to Manhattan to start her career, she was my life inspiration. While my husband and I were separated, I lived in a month-to-month apartment near her, within walking distance to her church where we sat in a pew in the back of the sanctuary each Sunday. Tears rolled down her cheeks when we sang about mercy. I pinched the soft patches of skin beneath my wrists and closed my eyes. She had been through more hardship than anyone I'd ever known, yet she greeted the world with grace and openness. We shared our secrets and our trust.

She started to complain about pain. She lost weight. She couldn't sleep. I received frantic middle-of-the-night calls. The doctors assured us she'd be fine. I knew she wasn't. I threw myself into care for her, grew exhausted and frustrated, and sank deep into myself. She was diagnosed with cancer. I curled up against her weak frame and squirted morphine past her trembling lips as she begged for more. She died within the week. Just days after her memorial service, I appeared in court to finalize my divorce. To say I was numb to the finality of what was happening is a gross understatement. I didn't have the energy to fight for much of anything and blamed myself for much of what happened. I decided I'd just start over. I was thirty years old, and I had lost everything.

I attempted to salvage the relationship from years before but still felt I needed to keep it hidden, and so became distant from my family and many of my longtime friends. It eventually fell apart. I gave up on the idea of being truly seen by the people in my life—flaws and all—and still finding love and acceptance. I stopped trusting my decisions—and myself.

I ached for conversations with my grandmother, who seemed to be the only person who understood me. A woman ahead of her time, she told me from a young age that all I do in life is based on choice. I could choose my life partner—someone who shared my interests and passions and who would support me fully in charting my own course. I had a choice about children; it wasn't a given. And most of all, my career options were limitless. In an essay about the day I was born, my grandmother wrote: "She might drive a ten-wheeler, argue before the Supreme Court, and even sit on the bench herself." It took losing her for that hope she held for me to really sink in.

About a year after she died, my heartache began to ease. I started writing again, emerging from a period of numb silence. I spent more time volunteering. I trained for a triathlon. I practiced contemplative prayer. I made a bold move at work and took an interim role running an entire division's fund-raising efforts. Through this move, I met a man who had been in my world for years but whose path had never crossed mine. Like me, he loved stories, biking, mountains and water. One of my friends affectionately nicknamed him "Dean Mountain Man." He brought out my best creative energy and met each admission about my past with warmth and understanding. But fear and self-doubt kicked in. I listened to the little voices that told me I didn't deserve anything good and that I should focus on career before love. I told him I couldn't pursue a relationship.

One frozen winter morning, questioning my choices and feeling more alone than ever, I dragged myself out of bed and picked up a book on spiritual growth. I read the words: "Pay attention to the small things today that could mean something big for tomorrow." Hours later, two women whose work in Nepal I've admired for years posted on Facebook that Elizabeth Gilbert had challenged her fans to raise $10,000 for their organization, BlinkNow. If they did, she would perform karaoke at a nightclub in Times Square.

In four days, her fans raised over $110,000. Challenge met, that Wednesday I joined several women from BlinkNow at Queen of the Night and watched Liz sing an impassioned rendition of "Total Eclipse of the Heart." Standing by my side, smiling because he understood how completely important this display of bravery was to me, was my Dean Mountain Man.

Months later, he cheered me on as I competed in my first triathlon, which also supported the work of BlinkNow in Nepal. On my bike in a grand thunderstorm (not Sandy-scale but enough to end the race early), I felt an overwhelming calm. I realized I did deserve big love and great things. It was my moment to harness my fear and to let go of the doubts that had governed my life. As Liz would say, *Attraversiamo*! Let's cross over.

Tour de Fifty

—

Robin Murphy

I n May 2010, I found myself on the bathroom floor, literally and figuratively. Bereft and bewildered, my soul reached to the Divine for help. The Divine answered me with a book called *Eat Pray Love.*

After the dissolution of my romantic dreams, I had taken to my bed like a fictional Victorian woman. And I began to read this book where a wonderful friend named Liz shared her story. As if we were there together with a glass of wine, she comforted and encouraged me. Her emotional experiences echoed mine up until the point she went from wallowing to wandering. I was inspired. That would be my answer: I could wander as well.

So I began to plan the Tour de Fifty. In honor of my fiftieth birthday, I would have an adventure of my own. I couldn't manage a European trip like Liz, but the following summer I would travel across the United States, by myself, in my faithful PT

Cruiser, Ruby. I would fix the broken pieces of my soul and decide, as all good bathroom floor club members know, What's next?

I had some trepidation about traveling by myself, but mostly I was excited. After raising four children, teaching hundreds more and caregiving for a chronically ill spouse, what might it be like to do only what I wanted to do? To eat when I wanted and what I wanted? To stop when I wanted for the reasons only I wanted? To see the things that interested only me? Would I even know what I, and only I, wanted? It was profound to think about.

I also felt guilty for leaving my youngest child alone with her father for an entire summer but fought through that feeling because I was desperate for change and growth. I may have been running from my pain but I knew that if I didn't run, I would die.

The reactions I received when I announced my plan varied. Some thought I was crazy for being a woman alone on the road. Others were proud and supportive. I was told I was "brave" and "courageous" and "strong," and I owned those words as part of my new identity. I prepared and packed but chose to leave much of the trip to chance, embracing the motto, "It's not the destination, but the journey."

During my first two weeks on the road, I traveled from Kansas City through Memphis, Tennessee, to Asheville, North Carolina, and then on to Virginia Beach. I had never seen that part of the country and was shocked when I fell in love with the Great Smoky Mountains. It was like coming home to a place I had never been before. As I drove through those spectacular mountains, I felt my heart crack open. I rolled down the windows and let the wind fly through my hair, my bare feet on the pedals and music loud as can be. I had never felt this free in my life.

I camped alone by Grandfather Mountain and hiked to the top in a raging thunderstorm. I saw the full moon rise above the Smokies. I ate local food and drank local beer and talked to locals. I visited beautiful friends and inspiring historic sites and the magnificent ocean. I listened to music and myself. I cried and laughed and learned.

I kept a blog of the trip, and this was part of the first entry: "What I am most happy with so far is my ability to really be in the moment. To be aware of the beauty around me and feel my soul settle into my body and begin to learn to slow down and stay there and be present. That is the first gift of this journey."

After leaving the Smokies, I drove through Kentucky, Maryland, Delaware, New Jersey and New York. Along the way, I accumulated a renewed sense of wonder, some radical fearlessness and strong personal boundaries. And I discovered that the best way I could care for my sacred self was to travel as much as possible.

Now, every summer I travel on my own. I've driven to Montana, Wyoming, Washington, Oregon, Idaho, California, Utah, Colorado. I've returned again to the East Coast. I've gone north to Chicago and south to Austin, all on my own with my sturdy Ruby. I've discovered house-sitting is a great way to explore a particular area in a more long-term fashion and just returned from three weeks in a tree house hidden in the Tennessee mountains, living by streams and lakes and waterfalls. Today I booked my travel plans to England, Scotland and Wales.

My life is now a prayer of gratitude. I know that no matter what happens, Nature is always there, supporting and inspiring me, and when I return to Her, I find the Divine. Reading Liz's story changed my story.

Recognizing Myself

—

Kitty Taylor

E lizabeth Gilbert didn't want to be married anymore.
Neither did I.
Between 2006 and 2007, I started *Eat Pray Love* four
different times. I couldn't make it through sixteen pages without
tears; sometimes it was only ten. I was married and miserable,
made more miserable by being twenty-six and barely one year
into vows I had written.

I promise to share my life with you,
    And to honor your life as my own.

But I hid in fear and sadness.

Knowing your kind heart, I will follow you.
    And believing in our marriage, I will grow with you.

But we did not partner as husband and wife.

Trusting you as you are,
  I will love you always.

But he had an addiction and I had an affair, though both are now behind us.

Pet sitting became my refuge during this time. Friends taking long weekend getaways and others attending academic conferences gave me the safe space to be alone and honest with myself and my furry company about where I was and where I wasn't.

One year after first hinting at my husband about my uncertainty over our marriage, I was still married and still struggling between truth and expectation. Thankfully, I had been gifted an entire glorious week in which I headed to someone else's home after work and slept alongside dogs that did not link me with another person the way our Lucy did. A curvy and joyful chocolate Labrador retriever, she stole our hearts when my husband and I moved into our first shared space. She had been the community dog, cared for by everyone on our road, but declared herself ours when she jumped into our truck as we packed for vacation. She moved with us to the cabin on the mountain where we were engaged and joined us on our honeymoon when we traveled to the North Carolina coast in perfect October weather. She loved the sand and feared the waves. She moved with us again to the home on the hill that I would eventually leave and where she would stay. She loved vanilla ice cream, taking up space on the couch and being scratched behind her ears.

Happy moments were the hardest to reconcile.

It was that one whole week alone and my first full reading of "one woman's search for everything" that invited me to fully grieve the truth of my marriage. I had believed that my heartache equaled doubt, that my tears meant reconsideration. When I finally made it to *attraversiamo*, I understood, gratefully, that just because a decision made me sad did not mean it was the wrong decision.

I could be sad.

I SHOULD be sad.

I was in this, too.

Sitting on the porch of that refuge with the book in one hand and a telephone in the other, I said it. Out loud. To him.

"I can't do this anymore. I want a divorce."

And I cried for the sadness as much as I cried for the relief.

Another year went by. I experienced the joy of living alone for the first time while also falling deeply in love with Eve. Genesis Eve. Mother of all the Living Eve. Paradise Lost Eve. Lover Eve. Sister Eve. My Eve. She, too, had made a decision that was both painful and liberating. I was thankful for her willingness to defy a rule for experience, for story, for possibility.

I packed as much of my life as I could fit into a 2001 Chevrolet Tracker and moved to Nashville, Tennessee, where I knew no one, to pursue the Master of Theological Studies program at Vanderbilt Divinity School. For three months, I slept on an air mattress, and for the first few weeks, I often cried myself to sleep. I made my two closest friends over cigarettes. One was a smoker; the other was kind enough to step away from orientation with me while I puffed apart from the crowd. I spent two years talking about religion and spirituality over bagels and coffee or cheeseburgers and red wine. I studied theology and people among Christian pastors-in-the-making, agnostic seekers of social justice, a Muslim drawn to chaplaincy and a vegan Jew. I converted to Catholicism, clinging to the hope that it, somehow, would be the fix to my on-again, off-again volatile and emotionally destructive relationship with the man who had shared my extramarital affair. As a Catholic woman, I wondered and wrote about Eve and Mary as mothers connected by the loss of a child. I served as a chaplain intern for children and adults at Vanderbilt during the same semester that I took one course on HaShoah, the Holocaust, and another titled "Death and Dying," where I sat beside two close friends who were falling in love. Their marriage is now recognized in all fifty states. I became an ally.

I studied biblical Hebrew and learned to say *"Adonai"* when a text read the name of God too sacred to be spoken by humans.

Adonai, a prayer in itself.

Add on I.

Another way of saying, "Please help."

I did a lot of that, too.

Almost anyone who goes through divinity school will tell you that it is simultaneously the best of times and the worst of times, a tale of the city where you begin to seriously doubt anything you've ever believed because you actually begin to study it, and a tale of the eternal city where, if it exists, you will share in joy among people from every tradition and no tradition because what is after this life is big enough for everything. Or maybe it's the tale of three cities, or four or five depending on your karma, and you'll come back to a new city, in a new form, because you're still learning. No one actually knows.

In the midst of this cycle of doubt and belief, something that I was coming to know quite intimately, I surrendered to Communion because it was beautiful, but I longed to take in the bread and wine from a table blessed by a woman. There is no body so broken as that which, in its essence, bleeds. And of course, that blessing is impossible in Roman Catholicism, which refuses to welcome women into the priesthood even as it exalts Mother Mary—or at least a version of her.

So I served it myself. I served Communion. A year after graduation, I was working as a full-time chaplain resident in a hospital run by a Catholic health care company, and every other Sunday I spent a few minutes preparing Styrofoam-esque wafers and cafeteria grape juice and praying over nourishment that would serve patients and families and nurses and techs who were tired and seeking comfort. I thanked anyone or anything who might be listening for giving us a place to gather, so we could embrace a short and sacred moment of peace. In a building where people died every day, we needed it more than we needed tradition.

I certainly needed it. When I responded to my first code blue on my first weekend alone and watched a doctor tell a man that his wife's heart just couldn't take it anymore, I needed it. When I held and rocked and cooed over a stillborn baby, I needed it. When I met a newly diagnosed, terminally ill man whose wedding plans had to be moved to the hospital chapel, I needed it. When I admitted to my chaplain peers that I was as close as I'd ever been to being hit by a man, I needed it. When I built a relationship with one long-term patient carrying a boy and a girl in her womb and housed in the high-risk pregnancy ward, I needed it. When I received the emergency page that one of her newborn twins was dying, I needed it. When I was asked to speak at the funeral, I needed it. When I realized that speaking meant leading the funeral home and graveside services, I needed it.

I needed to exchange the rules, the expectations, the marriage, for everything.

I still do.

The last thing I did to surprise myself was sign up for six weeks of burlesque classes. In 2014, just two months before I left (or knew that I was leaving) Nashville and four months after the heartbreak that sparked my deepest and most frightening depression, I learned the first pieces of shimmies and shakes and watched my body move. Along with my Delinquent Debutantes sisters, I danced in front of a full-length mirror and found myself loving the way the curves of my body swayed in rhythm. I looked at myself as a creation capable of embracing who I was and where I was going. In those rare and unguarded moments, I recognized myself as a friend.

Eight years after my first full reading of *Eat Pray Love*, I pick it up annually to relive the dog-eared pages and reflect on new insights. I have eaten. I have prayed. I am working on love.

Let's cross over.

Out of the Dark

———

Danielle Rhinehart

I picked up Elizabeth Gilbert's memoir in the summer of 2008 or, as I like to call it, "the dark time." And this wasn't just any old dark. It was the kind of dark that your eyes adjust to, so you don't even think it's that bad, until something (in my case, *Eat Pray Love*) slices into your field of vision like a sliver of sunlight through blackout curtains and you realize how much things need to change.

Once flagged as a "gifted and talented" kid, I was now twenty-six years old, bored and unmotivated, dropping in and out of junior colleges, bouncing from one dead-end job to another, and 90 percent sure I never really had all that potential people used to go on about when I was younger. I'd been through some stuff, like anybody, and I hadn't recovered very well. Sure, I was keeping up appearances, but I wasn't making wise choices or surrounding myself with healthy people, and I was dangerously close to accepting a life far less wonderful than the one I deserved.

When I began reading *Eat Pray Love*, I was sitting in my dingy apartment, which was in a bad neighborhood and wedged among the airport, the train depot and a major freeway. It wasn't the best place to live—perhaps the most blazing sign of this was the fact that it was literally on Elm Street—but I received free rent in exchange for working as the building's property manager (quite a deal in Silicon Valley) and, more important, I didn't have to keep crashing with my parents, which had become the norm as I bounced among apartments and relationships.

So for about a year I juggled my "most fabulous landlady in the ghetto" duties, a full-time receptionist gig to pay the bills (the property manager position only covered the rent), some awful online university courses and a deep case of denial. As is often the case with wandering souls in their twenties, I was looking for my life's purpose in the bottom of bottles, which I often drank in dark music venues, with people who didn't respect me or my potential. A winning strategy, obviously, and it was going about as well as you'd expect.

Thankfully, there are some wonderful people in my life, who tend to give me piles of books on special occasions, which thrills my inner bookworm, and I adore them for it. To this day, not one of them has taken credit for gifting me this particular book. They all swear they have no memory of buying it. I have no idea how it wound up in my apartment. It simply appeared at exactly the time that I needed it.

I read the first ten pages of Elizabeth Gilbert's journey toward self-discovery and heard my own voice echoing back at me.

I began shouting out loud in amazement as she would perfectly, wittily, beautifully describe something I felt deep in my gut. I texted excerpts to my best friend, Katie, who wrote back with the same enthusiastic recognition of this kindred spirit. (Where had she been all our lives?) I spent at least a dozen nights reading and crying in my lonely apartment, eager to get to the next "bead." I bought a journal and wrote, "I love you and I will never leave you" on the first page.

Eat Pray Love told me I was capable of making the drastic changes that would lead me to a better life. *Eat Pray Love* reminded me that I *deserved* a good life. That I could embrace joy; accept my body as a house for my spirit, not an advertisement for my worth; find peace in solitude, and find the strength to accomplish all of the above.

In the year that followed, much like Liz, I lost everything. The day after returning from another round of bridesmaid duty, I was laid off from my receptionist job. It was the first time I'd ever been "let go," and I know they were being diplomatic by calling it a layoff. I was a disaster, and I'm sure I wasn't hiding it as well as I thought. Then came more heartbreak, along with the depression that tends to follow unemployment wherever she goes. Four months later, I was laid off again, this time from my property manager job. This meant I was out of an apartment.

Suddenly I was back in my parents' house, sleeping in my childhood bedroom, starting over, again.

I was so tired of being limited in my job opportunities (read: receptionist) simply because I never finished college. But opening up my career options meant facing the demon I had been avoiding for years: my dyslexia. I was only four credits away from an associate's degree, but those credits had to be math credits, and unfortunately, my type of dyslexia, dyscalculia, is numeric.

On many occasions in my junior college stints, I would enroll in the math courses necessary for university admission, hoping to squeak by with a C- and get it over with, but I dropped or failed them every single time. My shame was keeping me from doing what was necessary: enrolling in an entry-level course. Going back to basics.

Then I thought of Liz and how she bravely started from scratch, trusting that the universe would replenish her funds and her life, just as Ketut predicted. So I swallowed my pride and enrolled in remedial algebra. I worked my tail off, and, to my own amazement, I aced it. By June 2010, I had earned my AA and was accepted as an upper-division transfer student at all four of the California State universities to which I applied. I accepted the offer from San Francisco State the moment it landed in my inbox. Given the state of my bank account, I knew paying for housing in such a big, expensive city was probably out of the question, and I'd likely have to spend many hours commuting to class while still living with my parents, but I also knew I had to go. Without even consciously realizing what I was doing, I set the wheels in motion that would lead to a complete life-overhaul.

The day before classes started, I went in to San Francisco to have lunch with my long-lost friend Sam who had been through a transformation of his own. I told him that I was planning to commute to school, and when he asked why, I explained that (for a handful of pathetic reasons) I just couldn't move. The truth was, I was scared of failing, and he could see right through me. He looked at me skeptically, grabbed my napkin off the table and, with a click of the mechanical pencil from his pocket, proceeded to analyze my financial aid package, finding just enough money for rent, *if* I could find a good deal. He showed me it was ridiculous to do anything else. He was right. I packed my bags and moved to San Francisco.

Miraculously, I found an affordable apartment right across the street from campus. My first class at San Francisco State made me giddy; I suddenly remembered how much I love to learn. I stayed in most nights, did my homework, found a part-time job, finally quit smoking and got straight As for the first time since before my troubled teenage years. I stopped going back to the safe bosom of my tiny hometown every weekend, even though it meant some of my friendships wouldn't survive the changes I was making, and let my old life dissolve into thin air behind me. It was painful but liberating.

Of course, no story would be complete without a little romance, and just like in the movies, I fell in love with that wonderful friend who wasn't afraid to call me out on my excuses and fear. Miraculously, he loved me back. In May 2015, I graduated with a master's degree in communication studies, my family, friends and wonderful Sam by my side. Life was better and brighter than I would have believed possible only a handful of years before, and I still pinch myself occasionally to be sure it's real.

When I think about the awful way I lost sight of myself and how I had to burn everything down in order to rebuild my life, I can't help but wonder if Elizabeth Gilbert handed me the matches. *Eat Pray Love* taught me how to devour joy, become devoted to myself and fall in love with growth. I am so grateful.

Un Pedazo de Pan Dulce, A Piece of Sweet Bread

Elizabeth Veras Holland

I was introduced to *Eat Pray Love* a little more than two years ago. I guess you could say I was a late bloomer. I was deep in grief after losing my mother and trying to get used to life without her. I kept reaching out for people who weren't there. I needed something or someone. I needed a lot of things I did not have. *Eat Pray Love* fell into my lap at the perfect time, a gift from my Higher Power to tell me I'm not alone.

My mother emigrated from the small Central American country of Guatemala to San Francisco, where she met my father on a bus. He asked her how she was doing, and she looked at him with a puzzled expression. He realized that she did not speak a word of English and so used his broken Spanish to communicate. A sweet but short marriage followed.

My dad was and is a roamer at heart and just couldn't settle into family life the way my mother needed. She came to the

United States in search of stability and a home. He eventually moved out, and I was raised by my mother and my two older half sisters. It was a Hispanic household, but you probably wouldn't guess that by looking at me. I'm very pale with green eyes and dark blond hair. I look like an all-American girl, and that made it hard for me to identify as a Latina—but I also didn't identify with being completely American. I'm bicultural, and I struggled with what that meant every single day. Who was I supposed to be? How was I supposed to carry myself in the world?

Men were always the easiest way to solve my identity crisis. If I could be sexy and attractive to a man, then that sexiness could be my identity. It didn't hurt that any attention was a confidence booster—a two-for-one deal! Except it wasn't. Because without a guy to validate me, I was right back to not knowing who I was. Whenever I broke up with someone (or got dumped), I had to have someone else ready to go. My mother would shake her head and tell me to give it a rest, but I just couldn't.

I was lucky to have a mother who was always there for me, day in and day out. I spent so much time pushing her away that I didn't realize how much I internalized her presence. She would shake her head and scold me for dating so much but was still there to wipe away my tears when the heartbreak inevitably came. Then one day I met someone who I fell especially hard for, who seemed to understand me in a way no one else ever had. I put all my faith into our relationship and decided to move to a new city with this love of my life, where I'd start college. It would be perfect.

And it was. Until one Friday, halfway through college, when I received a phone call from my sister who was spending time in

Guatemala City with my mother. A benign tumor had been discovered on my mother's brain. The fact that it was benign didn't give me any comfort. I heard the word *tumor*, and a numbness enveloped me. I couldn't pray, I couldn't do anything. I just had to wait.

That same weekend, she went into surgery to have the tumor removed. There were complications following the operation, and she passed away suddenly. Life changed in a matter of hours. How did it happen so fast? Only a few days ago, I had been studying for exams and preoccupied with relationship drama. How was I supposed to deal with the loss of my mother? I couldn't even begin to answer that question.

Instead, I self-destructed. I left my relationship (and college) so I could party and live the single life back in San Francisco. I used drugs to feel good. I fell in love again, this time with a guy from Germany who I put on a pedestal so high you would need multiple ladders to climb up it. Together, we partied like rock stars. I slipped into my old role of sexy party girl, but I was beginning to hate myself so much that I cringed at the sound of my own name. My mother was dead, and I hadn't appreciated her enough when she was alive. I hadn't finished my college degree. My German had moved on when he realized what a mess I really was. I had nothing. I didn't deserve to be happy.

At my lowest, I checked myself into a recovery program. I was drinking every day, and grief was overwhelming me. I handed myself over to the hospital and said, "I can't take care of myself anymore." I knew I needed help.

It was while wandering around the library shortly after being released that I picked up *Eat Pray Love*. I had heard of it, of course, but had never committed to reading it. Now my head was a little clearer and my heart a little more open.

The Italy section touched me the most. I was inspired by the idea that those of us who have suffered depression could find a big happiness based on small moments of joy. It could be a vision, a word, a taste that encourages us to keep going. Before Elizabeth Gilbert bought her famous three tickets, she sat in the bathtub of her home with a dictionary of Italian words and felt something. She wanted to speak this foreign language over a plate of spaghetti. That little dictionary represented a new beginning for her. Maybe I could also practice being good to myself through food and culture. My mother's culture. My culture. The culture that I felt so conflicted about because I didn't look the part.

I was broke, though, and in early recovery, so traveling to Latin America wasn't an option. Luckily, that's the beauty of culture. There are many avenues that you can use to explore it.

I started going to a *panaderia* in the Mission District of San Francisco that sells pieces of *pan dulce* and *pastelitos* for ninety cents each. With every taste of those little pieces of sweet Mexican bread, with every sip of Abuelita's hot chocolate, I could feel something in me coming back to life. The food brought me back to my childhood; it reminded me so much of my mom that it felt like she was right there with me. There were always regulars sitting in the shop speaking Spanish and watching soccer. They got a kick out of how good my Spanish was. "Where did you learn to speak Spanish, *guerrita*?" I felt at home.

Eat Pray Love taught me that we can all go on journeys to find ourselves, and we don't necessarily have to get on a plane to do it. I never thought I could find myself through a piece of bread—but I did. I realized that when I speak Spanish, I feel like me. I don't care anymore whether I "look" Latina or not. I am Latina, and I feel it in my heart. My savings account is now getting bigger, and Guatemala is first on my travel list. *Adelante.*

Darkening Gray

——

Susan Krakoff

I gave the man at the river's entrance ten rupees, and he gave back five under a paper bowl containing a small pile of flowers and a candle. Before cupping my hand around the flame, I shoved the change between my hip and the elastic of my skirt. Then I kicked off my flip-flops at the top of the stairs that descended into the river.

The cold from the Ganges chilled my legs like when I tiptoed into the Cheat River back home in West Virginia too early in summer. Because the sun hung in the middle of the sky, the brightness from the light gray shirt made me squint when I looked down at it. Walking toward the big rock in the middle of the river, I kept my gaze ahead, as if focusing on the rock would keep me from losing my balance against the current. My heels sank farther into the muddy bottom of the river, brown and gray water creeping up my legs.

No one made me do this. No one urged me to. When I

e-mailed one of my girlfriends in California about the letters and shirt my ex-boyfriend had sent me, she'd told me it would be funny to throw his shirt into the river, where it belonged. Now that I was actually here, it didn't seem like a joke.

A couple of months before coming to India for yoga teacher training, he had said he wanted the freedom to see other people, that I couldn't expect him to only want to be with me while I was gone. After dozens of nights lying awake in the dark trying to really hear each other through crying and yelling and justifications, we'd made the decision to walk away with love.

Inch by inch I stepped deeper into the river, looking downstream. The water flowed and nothing could stop it, not even my bare legs that stood firm like the rock in the middle of the river. The hem of my blue skirt billowed out and darkened, then sank down to my knees, as if heavy with the weight of my past two years with him. I didn't want to lose him entirely, and yet I knew that if I didn't unclench my fingers from the gray bundle in my hand, I would end up going back home in two months as if I had never come to India. The distance from him felt good, like I was slowly creating space for something new.

In the few minutes that I had been in the river, I'd almost forgotten why I was there. When I looked down at the paper bowl of flowers resting on my left palm, I remembered. I could smell the mustiness of the river, filled with dirt and people and gasoline from small boats. Closing my eyes above the smoke from the flame in the bowl, I thought I felt myself inhale, but no air came in, like the false inhalations we practiced in yoga class. I could feel my chest rise and fall, but it wasn't until I heard an *om* ring around me that I realized my lips had parted and I had been breathing the whole time.

I dropped my right hand into the water and felt the river weave between my fingers and the folds of his shirt. I placed the bowl on the surface of the water. The flowers that had seemed to fade when I bought them a few minutes ago looked brighter to me now. Making my chest tight, I clenched my ribs, released both hands and turned around to walk out of the Ganges, empty-handed.

Getting Back to Me

Tracie Cornell

It was 2008. I had just put my two children to bed (at the time they were five and twelve months old) and was now lying in bed myself. I did this every night: crawled into bed with the TV on, while my husband watched the other TV downstairs. We were experts at this dance—we existed in each other's presence but were merely going through the motions. I assumed this was normal, just what happens to a couple when you have two kids and two careers, you're tired and the marriage isn't new anymore. I thought everyone felt like this. Still, some part of me knew something was wrong—I just couldn't put my finger on it.

That particular evening, though, I had something to look forward to besides staring at the TV until I fell asleep. I had just started reading *Eat Pray Love*, after seeing Elizabeth Gilbert's first appearance on *Oprah*. I dove into Elizabeth's story. The scene where she's lying on her bathroom floor in the middle of the night, crying and asking God for answers, was pivotal for me. For the first time, I was reading about someone who was honest about her unhappy marriage. I wasn't alone! But could I admit that this was more than just a phase?

In the coming weeks, I read *Eat Pray Love* every moment I could. I read about Elizabeth's adventures, her self-realizations. But what really resonated for me was the decision point—the particular moment when she decided she could not keep doing what she was doing for one minute longer. It felt like a lightbulb went off. Yes! It *was* okay to admit that I didn't like my married life anymore. It was okay.

So often, women—in particular, moms with very young kids—give up on themselves. They think they can't change their lives and make themselves happy if they have babies waiting for them at home. But reading about what Elizabeth went through, her years abroad, created a door for women like me to walk through. It created a space for us to leave our unhappiness behind.

In the weeks after finishing *Eat Pray Love*, I started to be more vocal with my husband. At a wedding, I suggested we dance and he looked at me like I had five heads. After the wedding we went to a bar with friends; I looked over and found my husband across the room flirting with two blond women. I was mortified. When we got home, I told him how upset I was with him—and not just about his behavior at the wedding. There was a lot more to what was going on with us than a dance or a dalliance at a bar. At one point he said, "Well, what are we going to do? It's not like we can get divorced." I said, "Oh. Yes. We. Can." I could tell from the expression on his face that he didn't expect that from me. *Eat Pray Love* had given me the permission I felt I needed to let the word *divorce* fall off my lips.

Now I became determined to find my own voice. I started to make the shift from "I'm going to just stay in this situation and hope it fixes itself" to "I'm going to do something to change my life" because we have only one life—we better live it.

I didn't go away for a year, which would have been impossible with two young kids at home and a full-time job, but what I did start to do was to take care of myself in any and every capacity I knew how. The gym was my Italy, a weekend away with girlfriends was my Indonesia and spending quiet time reading or running or just going for a coffee was my India. I was about to enter into a phase of life where I was on my own for the first time in fifteen years, and this was the most incredible gift I could give myself.

I had a rough eighteen months ahead of me, and it turns out I didn't know half of what had been going on in my marriage (as Lily Tomlin says, "If you want to get to know someone, divorce them. No, if you want to realize you never really knew them at all, divorce them"). But one of the reasons I didn't completely lose it during this time was because I was already on the path to myself. It all started with this little book called *Eat Pray Love*.

It Started with the Flu

Lettie Stratton

The stomach flu is an all-or-nothing kind of thing. Either you have it or you don't. And one day in the middle of June, during my twenty-second year on Earth, I definitely had it. To make matters worse, so did my partner.

We both stayed home from work and, between bouts of you-know-what, ended up reading the entirety of *Eat Pray Love* out loud to each other. Luckily, we started feeling better by early afternoon. It was dinnertime once we closed the book, and, given the subject matter, we wanted pizza. Scratch that, we *needed* pizza. And not just any pizza—we were craving the mouthwatering, to-die-for kind, with fresh mozzarella, heirloom tomatoes and piping-hot artisan crust that Gilbert describes so well.

We placed our order and had high hopes of being sensually transported to Tuscany with a single bite. Unfortunately, it didn't take more than a sniff of the flat, oval-shaped thing in front of us for us to know—this was no pizza. We decided it was time to travel.

Even though I had a job I loved at a sustainably minded book publishing company in Vermont, I couldn't shake the daily frustration of being trapped inside for eight hours a day, staring at a computer screen. I daydreamed of ditching the desk and learning to drive a tractor, or at least getting some dirt under my fingernails.

Six months later, my partner and I had quit our jobs and were boarding Air New Zealand Flight 5 to Auckland, about to embark on a fourteen-month mission of self-discovery. This wasn't really about pizza, of course, even though that was what sparked my wanderlust. I was craving adventure, exploration and the chance to delve into things I'd always wanted to learn about but had never made the time for.

I wanted to find out if Buddhism was for me. I wanted to do more yoga and really learn to meditate. I wanted to read more. Write more. Visit eco villages and ask whether I could live like that. I wanted to learn natural building skills and decide if I was going to settle in the United States or another country entirely. I wanted to try living the way I'd always envisioned I would.

At home, I found it easy to make excuses for why I didn't do my morning meditation or my yoga practice or introduce myself to my neighbors or eat in season or buy only organic or even always recycle. I called myself a writer, but I hadn't written anything other than a few newspaper articles in close to a year.

How can a person graduate from an accredited university and still feel virtually skill-less? Sure, I could write a personal essay and discuss the works of Nikolai Gogol, but I didn't know a decent wood-chopping technique or which plants belonged to which plant family. And I could do just fine in life without knowing these things, but I *wanted* a life that required this knowledge. Part of me was scared to go after it, though, because it felt like a commitment. If I learned how to grow my own food and construct a house using natural building techniques and rely on hand tools instead of electricity—if I actually had the skills— then I would have no excuses left. I would have to dive in. It would be the start of being entirely responsible for meeting my own basic needs. And in the age of ease and convenience where success means being able to pay other people to do things for you, that's a scary thing.

Before leaving, I wrote myself a letter. Dear Self, I began. You're on the other side of the world, damn it! So enjoy it! Be vulnerable and honest. Be patient with yourself and others. Don't stop writing. Have fun! Above all, have fun. I love you.

During my time in New Zealand, I spent a month at a Buddhist center learning how to really meditate—and also learning just how much sitting could hurt. I enrolled in a monthlong yoga teacher training course and a yogic sexuality class complete with public, naked massages that we were not warned about. I did a stint as a bricklayer and built a mud brick house. I spent a week at an electricity-and-petrol-free Catholic worker farm. I attended a Kiwi/Filipino wedding, sheared a sheep bum, raised seventy bull calves and got a good lesson in patience. I dog-sat a poodle named Poopy, cycled the world-famous Alps 2 Ocean Cycle Trail, picked grapes on a vineyard and went on a quest for New Zealand's best *tom kha* soup (Baan Thai in Hamilton takes the cake).

I also got head lice; found a rat nesting in my backpack; endlessly butchered Maori pronunciation; killed a spider with a book of Rumi poems (probably not great karma); was unable to figure out how to order straight black coffee in a mug larger than a thimble; spent a three-day backpacking trip completely drenched, with no dry clothes or tent; got an irreparable flat tire twelve miles from my final destination after a two-week cycling trip; and usually wasn't brave enough to correct people when they assumed my girlfriend and I were just friends or, even worse, when they knew we were a committed couple and chose to refer to us as friends anyway.

Overall, though, it was the best fourteen months of my life. Because of this trip, I gained the courage to really go after my dream of a totally self-sufficient off-the-grid homestead. Now, back in the States, I've begun my first independent foray into farming, complete with all the trial and error that goes along with it—seeds that fail to sprout even though I sing to them; a sore back from endless weeding; trying to properly irrigate in Boise, Idaho's high desert climate; and an eighty-year-old landlord who comes outside every day and grumpily asks, "Is my corn ready yet?" Still, there's nothing like sitting down to dinner and knowing that I grew the food on my plate with my own hands.

These days, you can find me sitting on the kitchen floor stuffing kimchi into Ball jars, covered in beet-stained brine, or talking to my watermelon plants as if they were human. The farm is my new office, and my to-do list includes items like: build solar dehydrator, buy scythe and whetstone and research baby goats. My partner and I are searching for our own land in hopes of soon making our dream of that homestead a reality. And it all started with the stomach flu, a great book and a terrible pizza.

Seek Heal Grow

Jen Flick

E at *Pray Love* entered my life in the winter of 2008 and became a shining beacon of support and companionship when I needed it most. Liz's story didn't encourage me to jump out of an airplane or climb Mount Everest, but it did support my radical leap into wholeness and my agonizing trek to get there.

The year before I found *Eat Pray Love*, my calendar was filled with the words *chemotherapy, double mastectomy, radiation* and *complete hysterectomy.* There were other words, too: *meditation, visualization, affirmations* and *gratitude work.* My treatments and surgeries were brutal, and this latter set of words kept me afloat. What's more, because of them, I began to experience God and universal love in ways I never had before.

Raised Roman Catholic, I was fully aware that what I was experiencing conflicted with the beliefs I had been taught as a child. Still, I couldn't deny that these new practices felt powerfully right to me. They seemed to fit the nature of my soul. I rejoiced inwardly over my deepening relationship with God but was cognizant of the distance I felt from my religious roots. It was as if I had woken up one morning only to discover the shoes I had been wearing my whole life had shrunk in the night. Obviously, I would need new shoes, but I had no idea where to find them. Alone in my newborn spirituality, I questioned if such shoes even existed at all.

So, I did what most seekers do—I honored my path and continued using my healing tools while hoping that my proverbial shoe store would reveal itself to me. Each meditation led me closer to my inner truth and farther away from the dogma I had always practiced outwardly. As my path expanded, questions arose. What would people say if I wasn't at Mass with my husband and children each week? How would the neighbors react when they saw me sitting on my deck in full lotus? Would my children be able to understand and accept this change in me? Was I risking too much?

This is what I discovered: once I dipped my toes into the waters of my truth, any concerns I had over what others might think drifted away with the tide. I also learned that there is a vast difference between being *shown* a way to God and *finding* your way to God. My foundational beliefs had dramatically shifted; I had reached the point of no return.

It was with this mind-set that I picked up *Eat Pray Love* for a book club meeting that winter, and in its pages I found a glorious surprise. Elizabeth Gilbert rolled into my life like a luminous vessel and cast open the doors to my cosmic shoe store!

In the beginning of the book, when Liz writes her letter to God asking for help finalizing her divorce and begins gathering universal signatures, I jumped in and signed the list, too! Having collected cosmic autographs in similar energetic exercises throughout my cancer treatments, I had a strong sense of what would happen next. A few short paragraphs later, when Liz received the phone call announcing her ex-husband had just signed the divorce papers, I cheered for her and gave the book a hardy high five.

Later, while in Rome, Liz is presented with the concept that a single word can define a city or a person. I connected to her struggle over finding her word and began to wonder what my own would be. Just imagining my word lit me up inside. It only took two days for me to find my word, and when I did, I couldn't wait to share it. It was my proclamation.

On the night we gathered to discuss *Eat Pray Love*, I waited in anticipation for the moderator to ask us if we had thought about *our* single words. Nearly halfway through the meeting, the question finally came. I could barely contain my excitement. I felt quite empowered as I announced with conviction, "Evolving."

My disclosure was greeted with mixed reactions. A few women seemed intrigued by it, some seemed confused by it and others appeared entirely unaffected. Before, I might have been disappointed in the group's motley response; now, though, it did not matter to me. My joy was unbreakable and grounded in knowing my word.

We had just finished sharing our words when someone asked, "What was that white ash dream about in India? That didn't make any sense to me at all." A general discussion followed, which ended in a nearly unanimous consensus that the white ash dream was "weird" and that India was the group's least favorite section of the book.

Interestingly, the white ash dream was one of the most profound moments of the book for me, and I understood it completely. In fact, I had experienced very similar visions during my deepest healing meditations. And India was my favorite section in all of *Eat Pray Love.* I resonated immensely with Liz's plights and enlightenment in those chapters. Prior to my own spiritual awakening, I would not have understood the white ash dream myself. What a blessing, through these discussions, to see reflected back at me the word I had chosen. I was definitely evolving! I had taken a full-body plunge into the ocean of change, and the water was crystal clear and cleansing.

Eight years later, I am in vibrant health and I continue to honor my true path to God. I also make it a practice to honor everyone else's. My husband remains a devout Catholic, and I lovingly support that truth in him. We explain to our children that there are many pathways to God, and we want them to choose the way that feels right to them. Ultimately, we are each responsible for our own unique relationship with the Divine.

As a committed seeker, "evolving" has been osmotically woven into the fibers of my being. It's become part of me. I have a new word now, one that allows my spirit to roam free and breathe joyfully, while keeping my senses open to the beauty of each and every moment. My new word is *living*—full-out, no-excuses living. I kick fear to the curb every chance I get. I squeeze the nectar out of life's happiest moments, and I love the people in it with my entire heart. I take chances and laugh out loud. I strap wings onto my dreams every day and release them for flight.

My healing journey was predestined, drawn into the blueprint of my life, and so was my resulting transformation. Just as Liz reflected in Bali, I, too, believe, "God long ago drew a circle in the sand exactly around the spot where you are standing right now. . . . This was never not going to happen." I've found my new shoes and have stepped fully into the Light, honoring my truth and remaining awake to the power of my word.

Thank you, Elizabeth Gilbert. *Eat Pray Love* made me do it!

Coming Home

———

Peggy Bresnick

For my entire adult life, I did what was expected of me. I built a successful career. I married and had children. I bought a center-hall colonial with a big, unruly yard and formidable trees. I sacrificed joy for "appropriate." I compromised myself in order to satisfy everyone else, and I accepted that. My life was good enough. Only, of course, it wasn't.

I have always been a writer. Writing is how I am able to define who I am at any particular time in my life and save it so I don't forget. It's how I memorialize others, how I figure out where I am and where I'd like to go. How I tell my truth.

Writing sustained and comforted me through a lonely senior year of college. I set aside each Sunday to write. I'd work for long, heavenly hours, often late into the night. I loved these Sundays, alone with my thoughts and my words and the hum of the teal and silver Smith Corona electric typewriter my grandfather had given me as a high school graduation gift. I loved the sound of my own voice in my head as my ideas spilled out onto crisp 8½- by 11-inch sheets of white paper, and the sound of my fingers clicking away on typewriter keys. Writing was my bliss.

In the spring of 1980, I left my bliss somewhere along the Taconic Parkway on the way home from Skidmore. My life changed abruptly after college graduation. In many soul-crushing conversations, my well-intentioned parents dismissed my writing as a hobby and assured me that writing fiction was not a career choice. My parents told me that I'd be a smart girl if I got a law degree or wrote for a magazine or made a name for myself in public relations. I wanted to earn a good living. I wanted to be a smart girl. At twenty-one, I was old enough to choose a career but still young enough that I depended on my parents for guidance. I believed they knew what was best for me more than I did. Their approval mattered.

So, I gave up what made me happy. I became hollow. And I completely lost my will to write, even though it had brought me so much pleasure. I convinced myself that no one would want to read my writing. I convinced myself that my truth didn't matter. I didn't speak up for what I wanted. I became silent.

By 2009, it had been nearly three decades since I wrote in a journal or felt the warm rush of energy as I created characters and shaped a story, playing with words just because it made me happy. Instead, I had spent my entire adult life writing for money and to advance my career.

In my late thirties, I married and had my two children. I lost my voice in that marriage. I felt beaten down. It seemed dangerous to speak up. My words were like land mines, and I was never sure when something I said would cause an explosion. I knew even then that my silence was stealing years of my life, but I couldn't seem to muster the nerve to make a change.

Eventually, I got out. In a voice that was more of a shaky whisper than a roar, I filed for divorce. Initiating the end to my own agony was by far the most difficult—and the boldest—move I'd ever made. When he moved out, I was simultaneously relieved and terrified of being alone. I reflexively reached out to find a new man as quickly as possible.

This rebound relationship was disastrous, and I found myself in uncomfortably familiar territory, when I realized something wasn't quite right, but said nothing. It ended, but only because he grew tired of me, not because I stuck up for myself.

Still reeling from Rebound Guy, I picked up a copy of *Eat Pray Love*. Friends had raved about it, and the similarities between Elizabeth Gilbert's story and my own resonated with me—her divorce after an unfulfilling marriage; the way she got involved in a new relationship soon afterward.

I didn't have a clue what to do next. I was fifty, and I felt like I was starting from scratch. I turned to *Eat Pray Love*, hoping it might help me find my own direction. And it led me to where I needed to be.

I had stopped reading around the time I stopped writing. But I devoured *Eat Pray Love* in two early July days. I was drawn in from the very first page.

Elizabeth Gilbert tells her story with humor, insight, self-deprecation, sensitivity and immense courage. Simultaneously powerful and determined and vulnerable, her voice resonated with my own. It was as if Elizabeth, wide-eyed and breathless, had swung open a gate, grabbed hold of my hand and we ran together with our hair flying, down the dirt path through the woods toward the swimming hole on a hot summer day, giggling and singing and shouting. She showed me what I could become, if only I had the courage to follow my purpose and the conviction to see it through.

So, inspired, I sat down at my computer and just wrote. And I discovered my voice was still there, as loud and strong and clear as it was in my final days of college. It felt joyous. It felt like coming home.

ABOUT THE CONTRIBUTORS

Rebecca Asher is a writer, author and stand-up comedian. Asher holds a master's degree in new media journalism from Full Sail University and a BFA in theater from Chapman University, as well as being a graduate from the American Musical and Dramatic Academy (AMDA) in New York City. Asher's books include a children's book, *Little Mouse*; a historical nonfiction book, *Images of America: Keller, Texas*; and a soon-to-be-released political nonfiction book, *The Conflicted American*. Her one-woman show, *Death by Chocolate*, a coming-of-age story about dating, dieting and death, has played in New York and Los Angeles. Rebecca has acted, produced and written for TV, film and radio.

Lisa Becker has published creative nonfiction in *LA Family Magazine* and various literary journals. She took a hiatus from the film industry to raise her kids and found that motherhood jump-started her muse. Lisa lives in Los Angeles with her husband, their blended family and three rescued cats. www.lisabecker.com.

James Belmont lives in Madison, Wisconsin, with his two life partners Alex and Nick and their fur babies Buddy and Pistol. By day, James is an event coordinator and wedding planner for a hotel, and by night, advises small businesses and nonprofit organizations on social media marketing and content creation. When time allows, James reads a lot of Jim Butcher and Liz Gilbert novels and volunteers at his Wiccan church, Circle Sanctuary.

Melissa Bergstrom is a Boston-based actor, playwright and teaching artist. She is the cofounder and co–artistic director of The Perpetual Visitors Theatre Company, a company dedicated to telling true, uncommon stories and fostering human connection and community. Melissa blogs regularly about creativity and life in the theater at www.theperpetualvisitor.com.

Cara Bradshaw is a fund-raiser and communications professional who has worked with international nonprofits to address issues of children's rights and refugee resettlement, and in higher education to promote interfaith peace-building and community engagement. She currently directs fund-raising at a national nonprofit that helps homeless and low-income families achieve sustainable independence. Cara is a student with The Writers Studio in New York City and enjoys mountain biking and hiking with her dog. She grew up in Gloucester, Massachusetts, and so, naturally, is a lover of water.

Peggy Bresnick has been a freelance writer for twenty years, focusing on financial services technology. When she's not writing for clients or for fun, Peggy enjoys listening to live music and exploring the trails near her Connecticut home with her two children and her two big, goofy dogs.

A native Texan, **Linsi Broom** has lived across the United States and holds graduate degrees in both psychology and conflict studies. After breaking free from the confines of a government cubicle, she now writes, travels and teaches trauma-informed yoga. Her passion is working with vulnerable/marginalized populations. You can follow her journey at livingthesearch.com.

Tracie Cornell is a life coach, nutrition coach and writer. She lives in Buffalo, New York, with her husband and two beautiful daughters. When she isn't writing, coaching or carpooling, she can be found at yoga, on a bike trail or sipping a latte. She loves dinners out with her husband and friends and is constantly thinking of where their next vacation will be. Find her at tracielynncornell.com.

Karstee Davis resides in Colorado. This is her first publication. She lives for lattes, rainy days, books and playing fantasy football, and has an irrational fear that she'll die before she gets around to reading Proust. Karstee spends the bulk of her time with her family, to whom she owes everything and whom she adores.

Tina Donvito is the former editor in chief of *Twist* magazine. Her writing has appeared in the *Washington Post*, the *Huffington Post*, *Time Out New York*, *New York* magazine and *Fit Pregnancy*. She continues to enjoy hiking with her husband and son.

Elizabeth Duffy is a grateful alumna and employee of Caron Treatment Centers. She has traveled the world and now, at age thirty, is finally writing about her experiences. It is her hope to connect with other kindred spirits through her stories and to provide comfort through shared blunders, desires and adventures.

Chelsey Everest grew up in Portland, Maine, and received her MFA from the Stonecoast low-residency creative writing program. She currently teaches English courses at various community colleges and facilitates a writing workshop in the Kelly Writers House at the University of Pennsylvania. She resides in Philadelphia with her partner, Tom, and their puppy, Rue.

Jen Flick is a number-one bestselling author and inspirational speaker. She coauthored the books *The Wisdom of Midlife Women 2, Cultivating Joy* and *Unleash Your Inner Magnificence.* As an avid student of metaphysics, Jen firmly believes in integrating modern medicine with holistic treatments to achieve optimal health. Awakened to her true self after being diagnosed with breast cancer in 2006, Jen now lives a vibrant, healthy, joyful life, and her mission is to support others who want to do the same. Learn more at www .JenFlick.com.

Crystal Gasser is twenty-three years old and a current resident of Eugene, Oregon, where she's in college, studying psychology. Her interests include writing, getting out in nature, yoga and spending time with close friends.

Laurie Granieri's work has been broadcast on NPR, published in the Boxcar Poetry Review and appeared in the 2011 essay collection *This I Believe: On Fatherhood.* She lives in New Jersey.

Jan Haag is a professor of journalism and English at Sacramento City College in the capital of California, where she also leads weekly writing groups encouraging people to trust their voices on the page. She is the author of a book of poetry about her late husband, *Companion Spirit*, and she has written two novels—one set in British Columbia and one in Sacramento.

Aimee Halfpenny is a nonprofit professional who has worked on projects in Guatemala, Nicaragua and Mexico. She is currently the director of development for Mama's Kitchen, a nonprofit that provides meals to the critically ill. She loves inspiring others, having extra salt on her margarita glass and giggling with her family.

Alexandria Hodge has a degree in creative writing and English from the University of Nebraska at Omaha and is pursuing her master's degree in English education at University College London. At a very young age she relished the instructional and soothing powers literature had on her life, and she has dedicated her professional pursuits toward giving others access to that same sense of paradise. She currently lives in London, England, with her boyfriend, but considers Omaha, Nebraska, to be her irreplaceable home.

Elizabeth Veras Holland currently lives in the Bay Area and is pursuing a degree in Spanish and liberal arts at City College of San Francisco. This is her first publication.

Sondra Imperati lives with Michael in Rochester, New York. While he cooks dinner at night, she continues to pursue her passion for writing. They worship at Spiritus Christi Church and still sing with the gospel choir.

Kahla Kiker is a multi-genre writer who believes her purpose is to enlighten everyone that "you are not limited—you can chase and catch as many dreams as you desire." When she is not writing or working in her career in finance, she can be found shooting competitive sporting clays with her husband, George, or juggling the busy schedules of her three beautiful children.

For most of her life, **Annmarie Kostyk** has been on a search for meaning—and the tastiest foods available. She studied arts and humanities at Indiana University and has a professional chocolatier certificate from Ecole Chocolat and a certificate in L'Art du Gâteau—the art of cake baking and decorating—from the French Pastry School. She has published four books on chocolate, including *The Chocolate Travel Guide* and *Marais Chocolate Skin Care*. You can find her at AnnmarieKostyk.com.

Nosipho Kota is a writer and poet. She was born in New Brighton, Port Elizabeth, South Africa, and has worked as a communications manager for the Eastern Cape's Office of the Premier and Department of Health, as well as a journalist for the *Weekend Post* in Port Elizabeth, and the *Daily Dispatch* in East London. Her poetry collection, *Bare Soul*, was launched at the Cape Town Book Festival in 2010. In 2015, she founded her own company, Kota Communications, which coaches writers, with a focus on young women, and assists them with publishing their work.

Mallory Kotzman is a fearless reader and world traveler. She believes in the power of kindness and unconditional love. Mallory lives in Pittsburgh with her husband, Timothy, where she is currently working on her first novel.

Susan Krakoff is originally from Ohio but currently lives in Cork, Ireland. In 2015 she graduated from the West Virginia Wesleyan College MFA program in creative writing. She continues to write early childhood memoir and travel writing. Susan is a trained birth doula and plans to work with pregnant teens and Spanish-speaking moms either in the Midwest or Ireland.

Eduardo Martinez is forty-two, lives in California and two years ago started on the road that's led him to the second half of his life, embracing spirituality and welcoming maturity with open arms. He currently teaches special education in the public school system.

Nicole Massaro is a lover of literature who works in advertising. She has no previous publications, despite all of her mother's encouragement. Nicole lives in Greenville, South Carolina, with an engineer and a dog named Hadley. Greece is next on her list of places to see.

Leslie Patrick Moore is a freelance journalist and the author of two books about writing. She has lived and worked on six continents, and she's now married to the handsome Englishman Steven Moore. When they're not traveling, she and her novelist-husband call San Miguel de Allende, Mexico, home. Her website is www.lesliepatrick.com.

Robin Murphy, explorer; having completed Chapter One of her own life, in which she taught high school theater for twenty-five years and raised four amazing children, moves forward into Chapter Two, where the synopsis includes much adventure, romance, creativity and abundance.

Theressa Real is a single mom of three kids and a member of the military. She spends her free time writing short stories, working on a novel, painting crazy pictures, bending into weird yoga poses and laughing at the joy of being a parent. Most days, she can be found roaming the local musician's corner, gleefully taking in local art and delicious coffee.

Danielle Rhinehart is a music lover, animal fanatic and lifelong bookworm. She recently completed more than a decade of college and now hopes to explore the planet, relax a little and catch up on her leisure reading. She currently resides in San Francisco with her main squeeze, Sam, and the feisty family of raccoons who inhabit the palm tree in their backyard.

New York Times–bestselling author **Peter Richmond** earned a BA in philosophy from Yale in 1976 and an MA in teaching from Moravian College in 2015, and somewhere in there also flunked out of auto mechanics school. He has published seven books, most recently the young adult novel *Always a Catch* (Philomel Press). His work has been featured in fourteen anthologies, including *Best American Sportswriting of the Century.*

Billy Rosa is a nurse educator for the Human Resources for Health Program in Kigali, Rwanda. He writes a weekly column for the *New Times: Rwanda's Leading English Daily* on health and well-being, and his first book, *Nurses as Leaders: Evolutionary Visions of Leadership,* will be published in fall 2016. Billy collaborates with national and international nursing organizations, has been recognized with several awards for his contributions to the profession and aspires to complete PhD studies in the near future.

Sandra Roussy grew up in a small fishing village on the east coast of Canada. Having a teacher for a dad meant long summers road-tripping with her family, which sparked dreams of faraway travels. After facing her fears and starting a new chapter in her life, Sandra is now teaching, writing and photographing her way to those faraway places she dreamed about all those years ago. To follow Sandra on her adventure, visit: www.twelvehundredjourney.com.

Victoria Russell, a New Jersey native, graduated from Drew University with a BA in English. She has worked for the Brookdale Community College Writing Center and the Dodge Poetry Festival. Her word of the moment is *mulligan*. She doesn't play golf, but she hears it stands for "a second chance."

Amy B. Scher is the author of *How to Heal Yourself When No One Else Can* (Llewellyn Worldwide, 2016) and has been featured on CNN and in *Curve*, Psych Central, Elephant Journal, The Good Men Project and the *San Francisco Book Review* and was named one of *Advocate* magazine's "40 Under 40." Most important, she lives by the self-created motto: "When life kicks your ass, kick back." Visit her website at www.amybscher.com.

April Schmidt is a mother, daughter, teacher, writer, yogi, seeker, autism warrior and more. She is passionate about friendship, family

and sharing her story. April is currently blogging at www.thriveasyou
.com, where she discusses life topics and what to do with all these
doorways.

Emily Shaules is an actor and creator of Shift Bars, the world's first
organic vegan energy bar made exclusively with zero-glycemic sweeteners. She lives in Asheville, North Carolina, and is honored to be a
part of this project. She hopes her story inspires you to go for your
dreams and live your best life ever—you deserve it!

Regan Spencer is a recovering anorexic and addict, a relaxed yet
devout yogi and an aspiring writer. She battled an eating disorder
since childhood and abused marijuana, painkillers and alcohol before entering treatment and recovery, and today she seeks to help others struggling with similar issues by sharing her experience. Regan is
inspired by artistic expression, the beauty of nature and human acts
of courage. A native of Washington State, Regan currently lives in
Seattle and spends too much of her time searching for cheap international plane tickets.

Lettie Stratton is a writer and farmer from Vermont. She studied
creative writing and has since worked for two publishing houses and
a music venue, farmed and written for a variety of magazines, news-
papers and online outlets. For travel stories from New Zealand and
other writing, visit www.lettiestratton.com.

Laurna Strikwerda is a Midwesterner who now lives and works in
Washington, DC. She loves being active in community organizing,
interfaith dialogue and the arts, as well as reminding fellow Washing-
tonians to enjoy life outside of work. She has also written for *Sojourn-*

ers magazine and several blogs on culture, religion and conflict resolution.

Eran Sudds is a photographer, mama and postpartum depression survivor. She is the founder of the Good Mother Project and is passionate about making sure that other mothers and mothers-to-be know just how amazing they are, as both moms and women. She resides just outside Vancouver, Canada, and has a spunky, loveable two-year-old son and a very patient and supportive husband.

Kitty Taylor blends spirituality, feminism and a likely glass of red wine into nonfiction. Following graduate studies at Vanderbilt Divinity School, Kitty served as a hospital chaplain in Nashville, Tennessee, and found her writing niche as an essayist. Kitty currently lives and loves in the western North Carolina mountains.

Theresa Thornton is a semiprofessional vocalist who still has an office job. She lives in Queens, New York, with her two cats, who are her biggest fans.

Lisann Valentin hails from Brooklyn, New York, with roots in Aguadilla, Puerto Rico. A bilingual film and television actress, she has worked with Sundance-featured filmmakers and Golden Globe winners. A passionate storyteller, Lisann continues to write about her journey as a lawyer-turned-actress, reinforcing the notion that it's never too late for a second act in your life. Learn more at Lisann Valentin.com.

Shannon Sykes Westgate is the owner and innkeeper of Pleasant Valley Resort in Arcadia, Michigan. She is an interior designer, business manager, marketing guru, chronic multitasker and mother to the most amazing boys. She and her husband, Tom, live with their family in Arcadia.

Amanda Whitten lives in Fresno, California, with her two cats, Guinness and Gatsby. For the last eight years, she has worked as an attorney representing employees in workplace discrimination and harassment lawsuits. Amanda is also a marathon runner—she runs a lot and tries to do it quickly. She's also an avid reader, a travel addict and, now, a published writer.

CREDITS

Credits